FATE

AND

LIFE

FATE AND LIFE

WHO'S REALLY IN CHARGE?

MICHAEL ALLEN FOX

McGill-Queen's University Press
Montreal & Kingston • London • Chicago

ISBN 978-0-2280-2043-1 (paper)
ISBN 978-0-2280-2044-8 (ePDF)
ISBN 978-0-2280-2045-5 (ePUB)

Legal deposit second quarter 2024
Bibliothèque nationale du Québec

Printed in Canada on acid-free paper that is 100% ancient forest free (100% post-consumer recycled), processed chlorine free

This book has been published with the help of a grant from the Canadian Federation for the Humanities and Social Sciences, through the Awards to Scholarly Publications Program, using funds provided by the Social Sciences and Humanities Research Council of Canada.

Funded by the Government of Canada | Financé par le gouvernement du Canada | Canada

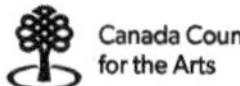

We acknowledge the support of the Canada Council for the Arts.
Nous remercions le Conseil des arts du Canada de son soutien.

McGill-Queen's University Press in Montreal is on land which long served as a site of meeting and exchange amongst Indigenous Peoples, including the Haudenosaunee and Anishinabeg nations. In Kingston it is situated on the territory of the Haudenosaunee and Anishinaabek. We acknowledge and thank the diverse Indigenous Peoples whose footsteps have marked these territories on which peoples of the world now gather.

Library and Archives Canada Cataloguing in Publication

Title: Fate and life : who's really in charge? / Michael Allen Fox.
Names: Fox, Michael Allen, author.
Description: Includes bibliographical references and index.
Identifiers: Canadiana (print) 20230550339 | Canadiana (ebook) 20230550347 | ISBN 9780228020431 (softcover) | ISBN 9780228020455 (EPUB) | ISBN 9780228020448 (ePDF)
Subjects: LCSH: Fate and fatalism.
Classification: LCC BJ1461 .F69 2024 | DDC 123—dc23

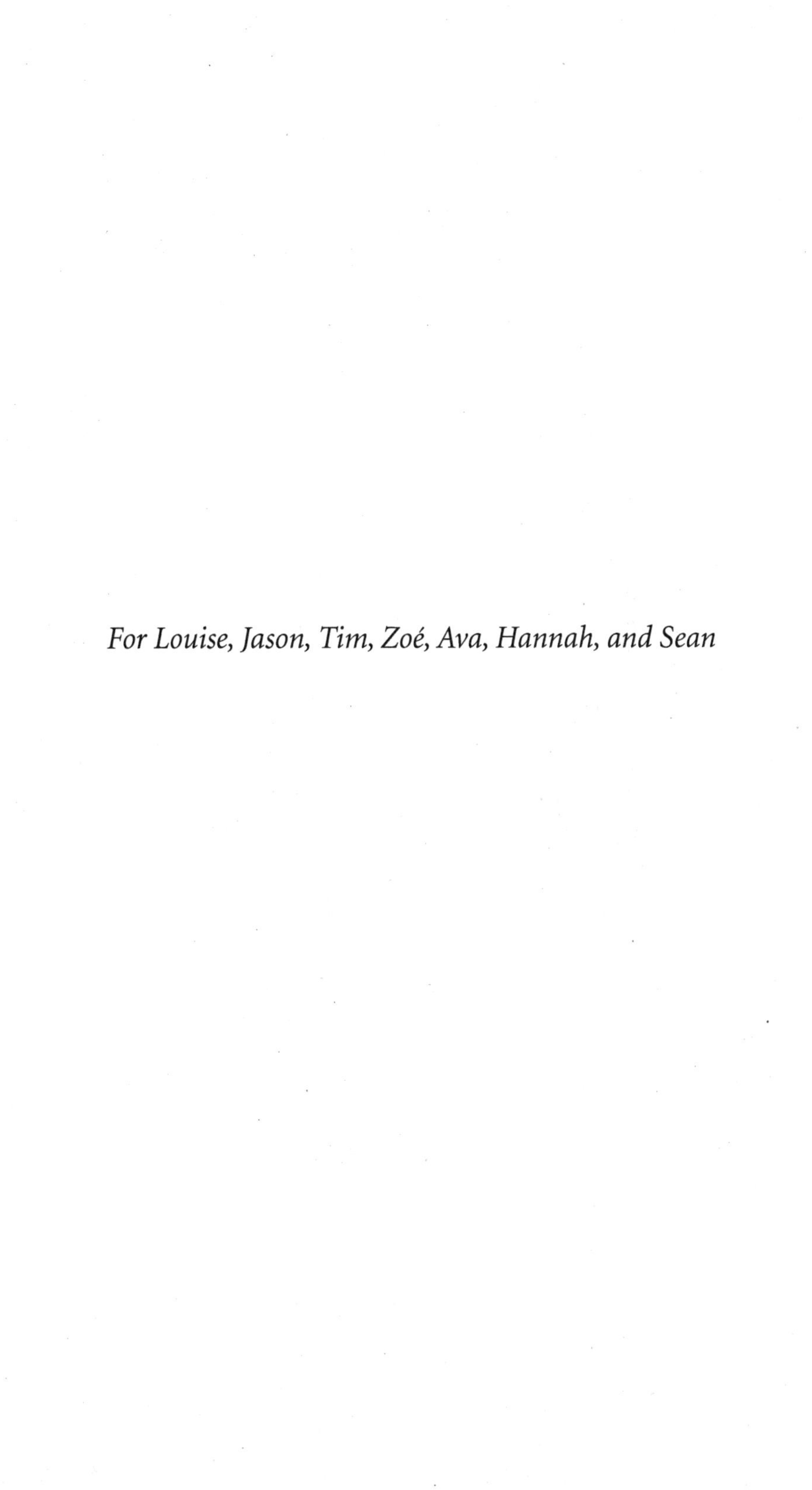

For Louise, Jason, Tim, Zoé, Ava, Hannah, and Sean

"Fear not," said he who had brought me this far,
"For nobody can interrupt a course
Mapped for us from on high"
– Dante, *The Divine Comedy*

What fates impose, that men must needs abide;
It boots not to resist both wind and tide.
– Shakespeare, *The True Tragedy of Richard Duke of York*
and the Good King Henry the Sixth (3 HenryVI)

No one created the universe and no one directs our fate.
– Stephen Hawking, *Brief Answers to the Big Questions*

CONTENTS

PREFACE

Our Current Situation, and What This Book Is About

We live in an age of apocalyptic thinking and rhetoric. Doomsday scenarios are popular themes of novels, films, and other cultural products that command our attention. This reflects the fact that we actually do have a lot to worry about, such as impending climate disaster, war, economic uncertainties, and the undermining of democracy. Natural catastrophes and episodes of horrific violence pepper the daily news and keep us all on edge. Pandemic is not just a threat but a reality, with COVID-19 still taking its toll in various parts of the world and other new contagious diseases likely waiting just offstage. The road ahead often seems dark and gloomy. But apprehension over what the future might hold is nothing new. Every era confronts its own demons and collective anxieties about where things are headed. The holy books of major religions include eschatologies – doctrines concerning humans' ultimate destiny – that lay out end-times for the world and predict the plot that will unfold as the hammer blows of divine final judgment rain down on all persons and things. Behind or beside all of this, everyone personally experiences the impact of unexpected events – both large and small – that shape the course of their lives. It's no surprise, then, that when people reflect on their existence and the paths they are following as individuals, they wonder whether life is under their own control or rests in the hands of fate.

The concept of fate, or the idea of fatefulness, seems to crop up everywhere we look in one form or another. And even when fate is neither mentioned nor directly appealed to, it often exercises a powerful influence on our thinking and our psychological and value orientations, all of which affects how we act in everyday life.

Fate drives the disturbing visions of terrorists and cultists, energizes the followers of millennial social movements, and endlessly inspires pundits, futurologists, utopian and dystopian theorists, and storytellers of all types. Discussions of fate have no limits of time or space that restrict them to a particular age, society, or type of worldview. Careful investigation reveals that *fate is a key belief-element in human life that continually reasserts itself across cultures and generations, giving it both ancestral weight and modern relevance.* We find, in fact, that fate is an astonishingly universal and malleable concept with broad intellectual and emotional resonance. This makes it a fascinating lens through which to view our sense of place in the scheme of things.

Fateful outlooks may vent themselves in extreme interpretations of the world and accompany tall tales. But more sober and reasonable everyday perspectives are also everywhere to be found and they are highlighted in this book. Fate will be viewed here not as a towering, aloof, and controlling entity or super-agency, but rather in a more limited and personally meaningful way. This view showcases a concept that comprises the fixed conditions of life and the imponderable impact that certain unanticipated events have upon the path we follow through time. Fate, then, has to do with the most basic things – the beginning and ending and the ultimate comings and goings of life. It also embraces the fortunes and misfortunes that are our lot, individually and sometimes collectively.

We begin by exploring in detail what fate is, the many ways it has been thought about over the centuries, and what the doctrine of fatalism entails. Then we'll consider how fateful ideas have influenced human behaviour for good and evil, and most importantly, how fate can be constructively integrated into our outlook on the world and our life choices. The argument of the book is supported by a multicultural, global perspective, and is developed with the aid of many literary, philosophical, and commonplace examples. These reveal the numerous ways in which fate has played a significant role in shaping the psychological and spiritual outlooks of different cultures, and in energizing the clash of ideas within (and sometimes between) them. Understanding fate reveals this idea to be a fruitful avenue for gaining a deeper insight into the history of culture, religion, and politics. It is a powerful concept that we cannot merely view negatively and dismiss but must instead confront critically and with an open mind. This is because the ways in which people incorporate fate into their worldviews represent an important and vital dimension of being human.

Summary of Chapter Contents

The chapters of this book stand on their own and may be read in any order. Nevertheless each gains enrichment from those that precede it, so sequential reading is encouraged.

In chapter 1 ("What Is Fate?") we begin our adventure by defining fate, investigating the origins of the word, and distinguishing fate from destiny, chance, luck, and other related notions. The view known as fatalism is also shown to be importantly different from determinism. Most significantly, we learn that even if we accept that fate plays a pivotal role in human life, this does not entail believing it totally controls what we do. A panoramic vista is useful in the quest for clarity concerning how ideas evolve and are applied. Chapter 2 ("Fate's Global Reach") provides this overarching standpoint by examining references to fate across a wide range of cultures and traditions. Some cultural visions have been completely dominated by belief in fate, as expressed in philosophical or theological perspectives or myths, and many more embrace fatalistic practices of various sorts. The love-hate relationship between organized religion and fatalism receives special attention in chapter 2 as well.

There is a great range of expressions and contexts in which we engage with fate. Chapter 3 ("The Language of Fate") documents and explores these. Many examples turn up in fictional writing, where some of the most profound philosophical and psychological insights are put forward, best expressed, and put to good use. But we find out too that even the more specialized language of science is open to fate's influence. Surveying the ways in which we talk about fate provides a good glimpse into the soul of this important idea.

Philosophical arguments for and against fatalism have attracted interest throughout the centuries, and have been debated with great intensity. Discussions about the viability of these proofs and refutations are still very much alive today in various quarters. As chapter 4 ("Fateful Arguments") demonstrates, the case for fatalism is not easily overturned, in spite of the nearly universal desire to downplay or ignore its unpalatable conclusions. This chapter also takes a look at self-fulfilling prophecies and the implications derived from doctrines of divine omniscience and omnipotence.

One crucial issue concerning fate and fateful ideas that is generally overlooked is their misappropriation by those who use them as tools of domination and oppression. Chapter 5 ("A Tool for Social Control") exposes several fateful mindsets that are disturbing because of their damaging impact on people's lives. These have the intent and the effect of stereotyping individuals and depriving them of their personal freedom. This strategy of demeaning and disempowering others works by focusing negatively on fixed characteristics that they actually or supposedly possess from the moment of birth. Such characteristics may be real properties (sex, ethnicity, gender, genetic makeup), or they may instead be purely invented ones (caste membership, predestination to either heaven or hell). Declarations about the future, doctrines of historical inevitability, and notions of progress and national destiny also provide examples of fateful fabrications that are or have been used to control people's behaviour and frame of mind.

Chapter 6 ("Attitudes toward Life") shows, by contrast, how fate can be incorporated into positive, balanced, meaningful, even broadening outlooks on life. Each of us has a given heritage, to be sure, but we also encounter events that are life-changing in unaccountable, often far-reaching ways. How we come to terms with these "acts of fate" is of singular importance and may be uniquely self-determining. The stories of several "heroes of fate" portrayed in classical literature and mythology are inspirational. But there are also plentiful examples of the transformations undergone by ordinary individuals when they face inevitable circumstances and work through them to their advantage. Fate, therefore, has the potential to become a liberating idea, as well as a kind of anchor for constructing one's worldview and life-narrative.

We end, in the afterword, with a few reflections on fate in a pandemic era and on the future of fate. Fate plays a big part in our historical moment, and it seems to be with us to stay. How we think about it, then, will continue to reflect our adaptability as individuals and as a species.

Fate and the Human Condition

Although fate seems at first glance like a strange and even obscure idea, a more careful investigation yields some surprising and intriguing facts – for example, that people accept and assimilate into their thinking those aspects of life that surpass their control and understanding; that character is built by how we react to and manage fatefulness; and that fate resides at the heart of both religious and secular belief systems of all sorts. Studying fate or "looking fate in the eye"[1] opens up many truths about the human condition. It helps us discover who we are, how we see the world, and how we evaluate the possibilities life presents. We can't ask for more than that from an idea.

FATE

AND

LIFE

1

WHAT IS FATE?

Many are forced by fear to meet
the fate they struggled to flee.
– Seneca[1]

"You know, sir, there's some things seem like fate. Whatever step you take,
in any direction, there it is right in front of you, it can't be avoided."
– David Malouf[2]

We are always in the cross hairs of fatal contingency and the
trigger finger is tense.
– Charles Foster[3]

Fate's Role in Human Life

"Whatever will be, will be." This wise saying has become almost second nature to many of us. A popular song expressing it first appeared in the 1956 film *The Man Who Knew Too Much* by famed director Alfred Hitchcock (1899–1980);[4] the song went on to capture an Academy Award, and then swept the world. Fate, the song's underlying theme, has occupied a central place in people's lives through the ages and across cultures, and it remains personally meaningful and of pivotal importance to a great number of individuals and groups today. This book explores a widely shared mindscape that includes fate as an essential component.

Some may profess neither to believe in fate nor to take appeals to it seriously, and that's all very well. Yet in the broad arenas of cultural perspectives, literature, conversation, and everyday life, fate is invoked frequently as an explanation for the state of things. During the overall span of human history (and probably during prehistory as well), fate has been absorbed into numerous belief systems and has thereby acquired a range of interpretations. God, Death, the Devil, mythical characters, and various omens and signs have assumed the guise of fate at different times and places. This widespread influence of fate may be explained by the fact that certain core questions confront each of us sooner or later, in one form or another: *Do I have a personal destiny? Can I take charge of it? Do I freely shape my own personal future? If so, to what extent? If not, what does?*

It's a normal sort of experience to wonder whether the direction of our lives is guided by the decisions and choices we make or instead resembles a role we unwittingly play in some cosmic drama. William Shakespeare (1564–1616) is but one of a great range of writers who've stated some version of the view that "All the world's a stage,/And all the men and women merely players."[5] Could life perhaps be a preconstructed narrative written by a remote and unknown hand, in which fate lurks behind the scenes, pulling the puppet strings? Alternatively, might the truth lie somewhere between the extremes of freedom and fate?[6] Fate might simply be the way things have turned out for someone, the sum of those important and not-so-important eventualities in her life that just happen or else fail to take place. However, we may question whether these are things we might have altered had we chosen to do so and had we understood our circumstances better at the time. In that case we might reflect, along with a character in a recent novel: "once we know the end of an unfortunate story, it's tempting to ask why its protagonist did not do better to swerve his fate."[7] But then again, as another author writes, maybe "we live our fate before we realize exactly what it is."[8] Or could fate simply refer to what will ultimately happen to an individual, to the world, and to the universe as a whole?

Complex interactions with the presence of fate in human consciousness reveal a profound ambivalence and existential insecurity regarding the events and circumstances that govern the way life unfolds. Both popular culture and the world of literary fiction provide plentiful examples. The extremely popular Portuguese singing tradition called *fado* (which literally means "fate"), much like the blues, concerns loss, lamentation, longing, and the deep, aching desire for irrecoverable people or things that circumstances have taken away. Fado can be traced back two centuries in Lisbon, but arguably has more ancient roots in sources such as medieval songs, African seafaring chants, and Moorish influences. Steven Carroll's novel *Spirit of Progress* yields a realistic portrayal of the way fate intrudes into our lives. Vic is a locomotive engineer who has managed to avoid service in the Second World War, which has claimed so many men like him. During the moments when he reflects on what he has personally experienced, he comes to understand that the malleability of his own life depends on unfathomable external factors. Carroll writes, "And as Vic enters the kitchen, the memory of the stick-figure soldiers and the fate that might have been his is still in his mind as he gazes upon Rita's round body, containing the child that might never have been made had that fate been his."[9] Another character in the same novel, Tess, the owner of an art gallery that is rapidly becoming nationally renowned, is less fortunate, so far as fate is concerned. She laments the fact that if her gallery becomes "an institution" in people's eyes, so too does she become one by virtue of being identified with it. "Is this her fate?" she wonders, "as she feels the weight of this inevitability slowly falling upon her." Tess observes that "institutions are not so much born as called into being," and in her internal monologue experiences "the tolling bell of the word 'institution.'"[10] She thus illustrates the individual who feels the smothering impact of fate as a kind of judgment and bondage. But as we shall see, this is only one side of a complex coin. Fate often exercises just the opposite effect, liberating people's creative energies. Not only that; fate also is seen by many as arbitrary, in which case even though it may be experienced as representing some kind of bondage, this can hardly be the ground for passing any kind of judgment on a person's character.

Some people hastily set fate aside as an illusion or as merely a pretext for evading our own responsibility – as in the case of Tess above, who readily gives in to feelings of helplessness in the face of perceived "inevitability." Dismissing fate, however, betrays a shallow understanding of its multifarious meanings. Belief in fate *may* serve as an excuse for bad behaviour, or as a denial of agency; but it does not always do so. Yet there are profound thinkers and writers who nonetheless draw such conclusions. Philosopher Arthur Schopenhauer (1788–1860), for instance, acerbically remarks, "What people commonly call *Fate* is, as a general rule, nothing but their own stupid and foolish conduct."[11] According to Henry David Thoreau (1817–1862), "Every human being is the artificer of his own fate ... Events, circumstances, etc., have their origin in ourselves. They spring from seeds which we have sown."[12] In a slightly different vein, philosopher and psychologist William James (1842–1910) states: "We are spinning our own fates, good or evil, and never to be undone."[13] Meanwhile, novelist Henry Miller (1891–1980) opines that "We talk about fate as if it were something visited upon us; we forget that we create our fate every day we live."[14] All of these comments convey the idea that fate is really just human choice in disguise or in drag, and therefore something *we* create and can only blame or credit ourselves for. It is the path of life each of us fabricates for ourselves on a daily basis from bits of action and omission. But while people certainly do relegate things to fate for which they alone are responsible, many impacts upon us and many turning points are neither of our own making nor even open to our comprehension. And that is the overriding reason why fate maintains its attraction.

In the discussion that follows, we will take the middle ground, neither dismissing fate or reinterpreting it away, on the one hand, nor taking it too seriously, on the other. This will be achieved by playing down the inevitability or necessity element that features in so many conceptions of fate ("things couldn't have been otherwise") and accentuating instead its chance element ("things just are how they happen to be, as they are given").

There's no doubt that fate weaves its spell at various points in our lives. We know that it is always waiting around the corner. Marwan Kamali's novel *The Stationery Shop*, a romance that spans Iran and America, is steeped in the fatalistic outlook of ancient Persian culture. Within the first few pages of the story, we read that not only does fate dominate the overall framework of life, it also rules over the sub-events of life: "our fate is written on our foreheads when we're born. It can't be seen, can't be read, but it's there in invisible ink all right, and life follows that fate. No matter what."[15] This belief-set does not overwhelm the plot, but it hovers continuously in the background as an essential and unsettling reference point.

Mysteriously, fate is unreliable – fickle and arbitrary – while also being decisive; it is a close companion, yet distant and inscrutable as well. One can never plan on fate carrying the day for oneself or for anyone else. Curious, then, that people should ever trust in fate – and yet many do. But such trust is given mostly when they've exhausted other possibilities, and rarely because of indolence or capriciousness. Trusting fate comes about when someone is looking for a miracle, a life-changing intervention of some sort, or just simply doesn't grasp, at a fundamental level, what sense there is in the course of daily events. Because of this far-ranging profile, trusting in fate has evolved into a way of life for many individuals.

Even entire societies have oriented themselves according to the fateful interpretation of omens, star signs, runes, fortune-telling, oracles, prophecies, and the like. And historically important decisions have rested on such portents more often than we might imagine or wish. The ancient Romans, for example, are well known to have utilized augury – the close observation of bird flight patterns – as a method of divination to reveal the will of the gods and therefore, to identify auspicious moments for different types of action and political events. Over three millennia ago, the Chinese consulted cracks in shells and bones for similar guidance. Indeed, such practices reach back much further in time and include diverse and sometimes surprising examples, like the examination of sacrificial animals' entrails (especially livers). These divination strategies continued well into the Middle Ages, and various beliefs in omens and superstitions continue across cultures to this day.[16]

Belief in any or all of these strange indicators may amount to mere groping in the unknown darkness and may seem unlikely to provide the answers people seek. And yet this sort of commitment does reflect the perfectly human need to locate phenomena within manageable explanatory schemes so as to create connections that aid us in navigating the world. Believing in fate helps create a stable framework of this kind. Many religious practices have been and still are concerned with bringing human action into harmony with a cosmic order that is believed to prevail and can only dimly be discerned. Life, in this way, is a perpetual enigma. Thus, to live properly or correctly is consequently a matter of trying to interpret various signs in order to placate deities or act in accordance with their will, and to adopt a spiritual practice that brings health and prosperity to the believer. According to the view that fate is an "unseen hand" controlling and manipulating everything, many have concluded that we are its mere playthings, as noted earlier, and that we delude ourselves when we think that events are determined through our actions. But from a more limited and disciplined vantage point, fate can be seen as filling in the gaps where verifiable explanations are either too hard to pin down or are missing entirely. As we proceed, we will look at some of the ways in which fate shapes people's outlooks on life and death. Examining fate and fatalism with the care they deserve reveals that simpleminded caricatures give these ideas a bad rap when in fact they are more sophisticated and richer in significance and application than is often supposed.

Reasons for Believing and Not Believing in Fate

Why are some of us are fatalists and some not? There are a variety of reasons. Adherence to fatalism may have to do with feelings of disempowerment, vulnerability, or insignificance in the universe. It may be a function of superstition or certain kinds of religious convictions. Or it may result from finding certain arguments compelling (see chapter 4). Belief in fate may even be empowering (see chapter 6). People might think of themselves as controlled by fate just because they believe that "everything happens for a reason." But without further elaboration or qualification, this belief falls short of what is properly termed "fatalism," since those who may reject fatalism also endorse the view that everything happens for a reason (scientists, most obviously, but also detectives, psychologists, historians, and others). And in fact, anybody who has faith in humans' general and inexhaustible ability to explain things will also believe that everything happens for a reason. There is nothing particularly fatalistic, then, about this claim. It embodies an approach to the quotidian world that most people share. We tend to believe that the universe ultimately makes sense and that common occurrences are rationally explicable. This might even be called our default position for viewing nature and the cosmos. If we take this a bit further, however, and fine-tune the stance a bit, we do come to what many fatalists believe, namely that "there is an inscrutable world-order," as one scholar puts it.[17] The desire expressed here is to find the meaning behind what exists, in other words to discern the order that lies beyond appearances or beneath the chaotic jumble of ordinary experience and the seeming injustices of everyday life. This kind of underlying meaning is what philosophers customarily call "metaphysical truth."

Whatever may be the case with respect to the present and future, most people are fatalists regarding the past. That is, most of us accept that the past cannot be changed. What is past is fixed forever. Philosopher Earl Conee points out that we might as well admit to fatalism concerning the present as well; for "If anything is in some condition at present, then that thing's current condition is fixed and settled." Thus, he suggests, "The present is too late to do anything about the present!"[18] In that case only the future would remain a realm of free, unfettered possibility. The haunting problem then becomes one of deciding how to establish when the future begins. If time can only move in one direction (which is not necessarily the case, according to some physicists and mystics), then arguably the future, in its restlessness, is constantly rolling toward us. (Or we are constantly sliding into it.) Tomorrow is the temporal horizon we perpetually stand on the edge of, like the place on a beach where the ocean's water, propelled by tides and waves, meets our toes. This means that the future is being ceaselessly transformed into the present and then immediately on into the past. The present, on this view, shrinks to an instantaneous point that flows seamlessly on into the past. In this view there seems to be no room for any alternative course of events. We might suppose that the future "freely emerges from the present" – or is constantly "becoming" – and we have all the concepts surrounding the notions of choice and responsibility to back up this stance. But such belief has not prevented some very intelligent minds from wondering whether the future is nevertheless in some sense fated to occur as it does, thus completing the circle of events that are set in stone for eternity. For they wonder how, precisely, is the future becoming? It may be emerging out of nothingness or from the realm of creative imagination and inspiration. But then again, the future might just as likely be a state of affairs that is a fait accompli, breaking over us like a wave or slipping by us as we watch like passive and helpless spectators. We will look at some of these seemingly counterintuitive arguments about the future in chapter 4.

Understanding Fate and Fatalism (I)

Fate is generally conceived of as either an abstract ruling force or set of circumstances, or else as a sovereign, supernatural power or mindful agency (often personified) that, for unknown reasons, brings about outcomes we cannot override and simply have to react or adapt to as best we can. Often thought of as yielding a predetermined destiny, fate may be linked with a total direction of life (of the individual, of the universe as a whole), which is already laid out and unalterable. The philosopher and mathematician Blaise Pascal (1623–1662) presents, in his *Pensées* (*Thoughts*), the idea that humans are merely ineffectual specks or pawns in the vastness of the universe. The cause of events is ultimately a mystery.[19] Certain strands of traditional Chinese thought, like Daoism (see chapter 6), suggest a similar perspective.

What follows from this kind of outlook? One author contends that "If the power of destiny is regarded as impersonal, it is impossible to enter into any kind of relationship with it."[20] But surely this is a mistake: Not all relationships are interpersonal (that is, between personal entities); and not all personal relationships with things that are not normally regarded as persons (such as pets or artworks) would necessarily be labelled impersonal. Even within the view that we cannot change what fate decrees, we nonetheless can and must respond to fate in our own ways, and these may prove more or less productive. This indicates that *choice is a crucial factor in how humans live their lives, even in a fateful universe* – a very important notion that we will investigate more closely in chapter 6. But it seems clear that we at least need to know that fate governs us to an extent, or better still we need to know what our fate is in order to respond meaningfully to it. And it's clear that our response cannot itself be fated (to occur or not to occur, or to be of a particular sort) if we are to preserve an element of choice in the matter.

This is a good place to set out a couple of basic points about fate and certainty. When we say that something is fated, there is no implication as to whether this outcome is known in specific detail or merely stated but otherwise unknown. For example, it might be disclosed to an individual that she will meet the person of her dreams. But this is quite different from being told she will meet this person on a particular date, at such-and-such a time, in an identifiable country and city, what the person will look like and say, and so on. Generally, fateful forecasts are oblique, vague, open to interpretation, and may be partly or even wholly symbolic. Perhaps, though, this feature owes more to the character of traditional narratives around fate than to how we actually encounter fate in our own lives. Personal engagement with fate tends to be direct, revelatory, and striking. It is, as we say, "a fateful experience." And it takes the form either of a lesson learned ("I guess that's just the way things have panned out") or of a revelation ("Nothing could have prepared me for an act of grace or good fortune like this"). The following true story is a case in point. Professional tennis player Diego Schwartzman relates that his Jewish maternal great-grandfather and a number of others made a fortuitous escape from a train bound for a Polish concentration camp during the Holocaust of the Second World War: "The coupling that connected two of the train's cars somehow broke. Part of the train kept going, and the other stayed behind. That allowed for everyone trapped inside … to run for their lives … Just thinking about it makes me realize how lives can change in a heartbeat." His escapee relative later managed to bring his family to safety in Argentina, where they began new personal histories.[21]

Perhaps we now confront an additional characteristic of fate: that the quality of its impacts appears to be random, arbitrary, and vagarious. It follows from this that many people, when pondering the deliverances of fate (and similarly, of luck or fortune), have a sense of unfairness or unjustifiability about these outcomes. A character in Jérôme Ferrari's novel *The Sermon on the Fall of Rome*, for instance, angrily hangs up the phone on her annoying uncle, "cursing the cruel injustice of a fate that had seen fit to deprive her of her own parents while taking good care to spare this intolerable old fart." Another Ferrari character is "a clumsy, uneducated peasant whom fate had catapulted into a world he did not merit."[22] "Fate," as philosopher Michael Gelven observes more generally, "rains upon the just and the unjust" in equal measure.[23] According to Gelven at least, fate obeys no rules and no moral appraisal is embedded in its operation. Fate follows no fairness principle that ensures appropriate or proportionate rewards and punishments; indeed there are no rules at all to describe its dispensations, whether good or bad. We can say then that the arbitrariness of fate mirrors the way of the world more generally. This is one of the primary reasons for calling on fate – or alternatively believing in a supernatural deity – to rationalize the unfairness of life. Taking a long view, however, Gelven argues that rather than limiting us, appeals to fate open a way for our individual lives to matter, because we define ourselves by the way we respond to our lot. This idea will bear fruit as we proceed – provided we endorse and actively affirm the position that fate is not an all-encompassing master of our existence.

A somewhat different line is taken by those who see fate as somehow consolidating or giving wholeness to our lives. In Niall Williams' novel *This Is Happiness*, the narrator muses that "it's only after a thing happens that you realize you knew it was going to."[24] Likewise, Isabel Allende's character Violeta, in her novel of the same name, observes that "Sometimes our fates take turns that we don't notice in the moment they occur, but … they become clear in hindsight."[25] This is the backward-looking spirit in which one says that a chance encounter (such as a romantic liaison, for example) was "meant to happen." But it also reflects the attitude that fate is a bolt from the blue – a phenomenon that resides outside of the usual causal order of things, which we cannot expect to manifest in any predictable way. and the action of which is indifferent to our individual agency. We should be cautious about taking this approach too often, though, since if we allow it to dominate our outlook it becomes quite disempowering. Fate does not (or need not) dominate our lives. It is just one of the raw materials from which we put together our individual narratives.

Understanding Fate and Fatalism (II)

We can now take a closer and more precise look at the meaning of fate. The English word "fate" derives from the Latin *fatum*, itself derived from the Latin *fari*, meaning "to say." Thus, we can understand why expressions such as "It is said that" or "So sayeth the Lord" or "Ancient wisdom is expressed in sayings like …" possess the flavour of fateful utterances. For if a supremely powerful or revered being makes a pronouncement, then what is spoken seems bound to happen or to prevail. The strength of the words and the especially inspired speaker – for instance an elder, oracle, or deity – ensures it. As we are told in the Bible, "By the word of the Lord were the heavens made; and all the host of them by the breath of his mouth"; "And God said, Let there be light: and there was light."[26] Even the inventions of popular culture – such as the world depicted by J.R.R. Tolkien (1892–1973) in *Lord of the Rings* or the realms of fantasy comic book superheroes – feature the power of statements to bring about events. Who can forget *Star Trek*'s Captain Jean-Luc Picard, played by Sir Patrick Stewart, issuing orders with a pointed finger and the words "Engage!" or "Make it so!" Meanwhile, performative expressions like "I give you my word that this will be done" or "I promise you we will catch the killer," also carry something of the same force. Interestingly – and somewhat forebodingly – the words "fatal" and "fatality" have the same etymology as "fate."

Standard definitions of fate and fatalism tend to be rigid and thus fail to capture the nuances of meaning that we are after in this discussion. One such definition, for instance, identifies fatalism with "the view that we are powerless to do anything other than what we actually do."[27] Another equates fatalism with the belief that "whatever happens is and always was unavoidable."[28] A third version describes fatalism as "the belief that people cannot change the way events will happen and that events, especially bad ones, cannot be avoided."[29] What is lacking in these definitions? Three things, actually. The first, as pointed out earlier, is that they treat fate as a global ruling force or agency, whereas it may be that fate – if it "controls" anything at all – only partially or intermittently intervenes in our lives. Some believers in fate have even held that they could negotiate or bargain with it for more favourable outcomes. The model for this is Faust, who makes a deal with the Devil, exchanging his soul for the power to obtain unlimited knowledge and pleasure. This cautionary German tale was later captured in a well-known opera by Charles Gounod (1818–1893) and in literary works by Christopher Marlowe (1564–1593), Johann von Goethe (1749–1832), Thomas Mann (1875–1955), and others.[30]

Second, in certain fatalistic views – whether fate is a total or only episodic influence on our lives – we still retain the capacity to develop our own emotional and cognitive outlook with respect to it, as chapter 6 will demonstrate. Fatalism is often associated with gloom and doom, helplessness, passivity, and resignation. But belief in fate does not necessarily entail a philosophy of impotence and despair. People attribute their good just as much as their bad fortune to fate. And most who believe in fate do not appear to consider themselves locked into a rigid worldview where there is no room to maneuver. It follows, then, that despondent definitions of fatalism miss the mark. Defeatism is not a universal stance among believers in fate, and it is far from the end of the matter in terms of how believers accept and respond to what they feel fate's role is in their lives.

Third, these definitions equate fate with an irrational component of the universe, in relation to which humans are unfree. More accurately, however, fate represents what lies beyond the limits of human understanding and the vast complexity of the factors that govern both our existence and everything that takes place in the world. What we see, then, when we examine fate and fatalism closely, is that people view them with a greater degree of discrimination and circumspection than do the authors of abstract dictionaries, encyclopedia definitions, or most philosophical theorists.

Fate and Related Concepts

Several notions tend to be used interchangeably: destiny, chance (or coincidence), luck, fortune, karma, and causation. But there are important, sometimes subtle, differences between these ideas that should be identified and respected.

Destiny

Destiny, though often equated with fate or at least treated as a kind of sister notion, is nonetheless a significantly different concept. On the individual level, the word "destiny" identifies a path in life that is thought to be somehow "set" by one's natural talents, social class, or some other major factor. It is a beacon that one must follow.[31] Yet within the rhetoric of "self-realization," the notion predominates that, despite others' expectations, people should seize control of their own destinies. This outlook has been dramatically expressed, for instance, in *Defy Your Destiny*, a poignant memoir by Eritrean refugee Fiori Giovanni, which details her escape from arranged marriage and recruitment as a child soldier, and then follows her trials and tribulations as she crosses the world seeking a better life.[32] In a more whimsical vein, novelist S.G. Browne personifies Fate and Destiny in a narrative that depicts their separate roles in human life and the attraction and repulsion existing between them.[33]

A person's apparent destiny may, "of its own accord," fail to be realized owing to inaction. (And we may even think that some destinies ought not to be realized, if doing so is likely to lead to harmful consequences for oneself or others.) This further demonstrates that destiny and fate are different concepts, for destiny is open to enactment (or rather: requires engaged enactment), whereas the unfolding of fate is supposed to be inexorable and beyond our control.

Chance, Luck, Fortune, Karma, and Causality

Someone might object: "But isn't all this fate stuff merely a matter of happenstance, fortuitousness, or serendipity?" This view may be tempting; however, as we'll see shortly, chance can be as difficult to comprehend as fate. Chance events are often thought of as those for which there is a statistical probability, ranging from large to miniscule, of their occurrence at a given time and place, or under particular conditions (or both). In the personal sphere, such events are indeed plentiful (getting cancer or smoking but avoiding cancer; being born with a certain eye colour; living to age ninety-five or dying at age thirty-five). Other chance events, however, seem to have no likelihood that is calculable. These might include things like finding a million dollars on a park bench versus finding nothing of value there, or meeting the partner of your dreams versus living your life alone. And if it would take an all-knowing genius, limitless AI machine, or God-like mind to calculate the odds in these cases, then calling them chance events rather than fated events advances us no further in the search for understanding.

In the classic detective novel *The Maltese Falcon* by Dashiell Hammett (1894–1961) the protagonist, Sam Spade, tells us about Flitcraft, a man who experiences a near-fatal incident that changes his entire life. Leaving work for lunch one day, Flitcraft is just walking by a construction site, when a beam falling onto the sidewalk barely misses him. He never returns to work, disappears, and only years later resurfaces in a new location, having changed his name, and is found to be carrying on a completely new set of life-activities. Flitcraft interpreted the falling beam as a message from the universe that "Life could be ended for him at random," and therefore, "he would change his life at random by simply going away," leaving his wife, family, and job without giving notice to anyone. Spade's wry comment on this episode is that Flitcraft had "adjusted himself to beams falling, and then no more of them fell, and he adjusted to them not falling."[34]

The lesson here seems to be that one's lot may be determined by totally arbitrary, random, accidental circumstances, and that no life situation is inherently stable or entirely to be trusted. Is it really a matter of chance that Flitcraft experiences what he does? In a way, yes. And maybe the probability of a beam falling and barely missing someone at a construction site – perhaps even at this particular construction site – could be calculated, though that stretches our credulity quite a bit. But what about the probability of its being specifically Flitcraft who would be the unfortunate passer-by at precisely the given moment? The odds are incalculable. This is partly because the total number of factors that would have to be considered is astronomical (including, for example, how long he spent putting on his jacket, or brushing his teeth, or kissing his wife goodbye before going to work). Furthermore, probability calculations do not offer predictions about any particular identifiable individual, only about the possibility that a member of a class or group (such as "people of such-and-such-an-age with such-and-such-a-condition or engaging in such-and-such an occupation") will experience a certain outcome.

Here we enter the realm of fate. We don't necessarily need to say that Flitcraft was chosen or singled out by the universe (although he felt he had been), or that some malicious power held him in thrall. If he had been killed, we could have said that at that moment "his number was up" or "his fate was sealed" by the event in question. Would it be helpful to do so? Well, the answer to this question is, in a way, the whole subject of the present book: a meditation on fate. But briefly, it can be replied that for many people, at any rate, it makes more sense to talk of fate here than of probability and mere chance. Certainly, from Flitcraft's perspective, if he hadn't survived this incident, he would have been randomly nailed by a force or forces beyond his (or anyone's) knowledge or control; yet surviving them is just as mysterious and portentous. Some might even say to a person like Flitcraft: "Fate has allowed you a second chance" or "You've just used up one of your nine lives, buddy!"

Philosopher Richard Taylor (1919–2003), one of the most important and prolific writers on fate in recent times, observes that people tend to overlook the fact that "the entire course of their lives is often set, once and for all, by the most trivial incidents, which they did not produce and could not even have foreseen."[35] This truth is exceptionally well illustrated by Flitcraft's story. Taylor's way of putting his point underlines the fact that the path we take at many forks in the road is the result of freakish or singular circumstances – that chance plays a large role in the way lives unfold. Most of us do realize this if we think carefully about the matter, and would therefore (if content with the outcome of our lives up to now) not wish crucial events of the past to have turned out any other way than they did.

But the element of fortuitousness in life is much more broad ranging than we have seen thus far. One reason for this is that experiences – most of which can't be anticipated, nor their quality predicted – are instrumental in making people who they are. In addition, complex genetic factors enter into the picture, such as which sperm and egg combine to make you, chance mutations, and inclusion in your makeup of cells from parents, grandparents, or even older siblings.[36] The shaping of a life depends on so many completely incalculable conditions that, taking all factors and possibilities into account, your existence as who you are (or have come to be) is "vanishingly improbable," as one author posits.[37]

Luck is another way of looking at unanticipated or random events. Luck amounts to coincidental circumstances that either harm or benefit a person. When we observe that someone died of a heart attack suddenly and without warning, we aren't claiming that there's no medical or causal explanation of the event, even if it is unknown to anyone in the moment or even if cardiac arrest would have seemed highly unlikely in this case (because of the person's fitness level or other factors). But we might think it unlucky that such an individual was the one for whom this set of conditions – no doubt present in comparable others – led to premature death. Maybe that's just what we mean when we speak of "bad luck" – namely, a situation where one is not "beating the odds." But luck is often good too, and "being lucky" of course suggests having positive rather than negative outcomes in one's life (this is sometimes characterized as "being smiled on by Lady Luck"). Occasionally someone wins the big lottery jackpot or rolls the dice perfectly. Generally we don't try to explain this kind of luck scientifically or mathematically, except perhaps to note the size of the ticket pool and the ticketholder's chances relative to that, or to cite some wildly improbable rate of success at dice-rolling. Being the person who triumphs "against all odds" in a game of chance is a matter of pure luck, we may suppose – like happening to be at the right place at the right time to receive a benefit or blessing, such as being able to take advantage of an unadvertised sale or to see a beautiful rainbow. "Being lucky" is often equated with being fortunate or having overall success in life, while "being unlucky" or "out of luck" references being unfortunate or being the subject of misfortune. In any event, both good and bad luck hinge on given conditions that render people incapable of avoiding particular outcomes. So perhaps, in the end, "luck" is nothing more than a particular way of looking at or characterizing fate.

A metaphor and visual image that has crystallized the idea of luck as a determinant of life and of our state of happiness or unhappiness is the "wheel of fortune." In ancient thought and tradition, and in the millennia to follow, regular, repetitive features of the world and of the cosmos, such as the seasons and the signs of the zodiac, have been portrayed as forming circular, revolving patterns of endless duration. The concept of fate entered Hinduism at a very early stage, and by the time the great Sanskrit epic poem the *Mahabharata* was written (c. 200 BCE–400 CE), the god Vishnu became featured as one who "controls the Wheel of Time … the immense temporal cycle of creation (activity) and destruction (quiescence)."[38] The Aztecs also had a wheel of time, a master calendar, which likewise charted cycles of creation and destruction.[39] More than a millennium later, in Shakespeare's play *Henry V*, a brave soldier is said to be the victim of "cruel fate/And giddy Fortune's furious fickle wheel."[40] The wheel of fortune also figures in Boethius (c. 480–524), *The Consolation of Philosophy*, Dante (c. 1265–1321), *The Divine Comedy* ("Hell," Canto 15), and *The Monk's Tale*, part of the late-fourteenth-century *Canterbury Tales* by Geoffrey Chaucer (1343–1400), while several hundred years later a painting titled *The Wheel of Fortune* became a well-known work by the Pre-Raphaelite painter Edward Burne-Jones (1833–1898). Today's casino roulette wheel is but a pale shadow of these cultural precursors.

Luck shades into fortune, which in turn shades into destiny. In Chinese traditional thought, "Fate [*ming*] cannot be changed; it is set before birth. But fortune is amenable to manipulation. Bad luck can be avoided and good fortune be made to flow your way."[41] This doctrine strongly suggests that we are the agents of our own doing and undoing, even though our efforts may be faltering and imperfect.

Along similar lines, karma must also be distinguished from fate, despite some superficial resemblance. In certain strands of Hindu religion and philosophy, karma is the ultimate moral weight that our actions, speech, and thoughts carry and accumulate throughout life. Since reincarnation is also part of this belief system, it is considered natural that the good or bad effects caused by an agent will revisit them in some form in the distant future, causing either happiness (good karma) or suffering (bad karma). This appears to entail that we have no control over the good or bad fortune that visits us (and perhaps over the life-form in which we will next be embodied). Whatever happens to or befalls us turns out to be, according to some cosmic order or other, merely "what we deserve." But many spokespersons in this tradition argue that karma can be either enhanced, modified, or reversed. And according to some learned teachers a dedicated, purifying spiritual practice can enable one to escape the endless cycle of karma and reincarnation (samsara) altogether.

Fate is, finally, not the same as causation, even systematic, all-encompassing causation. Some early classical thinkers, however, thought it did make sense to equate fate with causation. Thus, for

Zeno of Citium (333–261 BCE), "Fate is defined as an endless chain of causation, whereby things are, or as the reason or formula by which the world goes on."[42] Cicero (106–43 BCE), writing two and a half centuries later, added that "nothing has happened which was not going to be, and likewise nothing is going to be of which nature does not contain causes working to bring that very thing about. This makes it intelligible that fate should be, not the 'fate' of superstition, but that of physics, an everlasting cause of things – why past things happened, why present things are now happening, and why future things will be."[43] What we see expressed here is the belief that there is no difference between complete causal determinism and fate. Fate is simply remote causality and part of the natural order. We will look at the difference between determinism and fatalism next. But for the moment, it suffices to observe the following: fate obviously makes things happen; but that doesn't render fate part (much less all) of the causal chain of nature, which is what science aims to understand and explain. So fate may be thought of as a way in which some things come to pass, but which we cannot in principle fully understand, control, predict, or even describe – though we can (and do) interpret fateful happenings and integrate these perspectives into how we lead our lives.

Hence we will say, in sum, that destiny, chance (or coincidence), luck, fortune, karma, and causation are all useful notions that have their own proper spheres of application. But at least some explanations that invoke fate are centred on elements of experience and action that none of these other concepts can fully encompass.

Determinism and Fatalism

The ability to choose is something humans hold dear and consider a vital token of their agency and freedom. Where fate operates, however, choice seems to be completely abrogated – though we shall see later on that this is not the case. Like fatalism, determinism also appears to negate the reality of genuine choice in human life. And since determinism and fatalism are often confused with one another,[44] we need to clarify the relationship between them. Remember that not everyone who believes in fate is a fatalist in the proper sense of the word. A fatalist is one who accepts the all-embracing rule of fate. And even some who do so (such as Stoics and many of the Muslim faith) still argue for the reality of free choice.

Determinism is the view that everything has a cause, and (according to some versions) that knowledge of scientific laws, plus the conditions prevailing just before or at the time of an event, makes it theoretically possible to predict what will take place. Note first of all that the belief that "everything has a cause" does not distinguish determinism from fatalism, since fatalists also believe this, although the causes they recognize may remain incomprehensible or obscure. So let's see what other factors actually differentiate these two concepts.

We do make choices, determinists think, but our choices are not up to us to pick out of the blue, as we might suppose. Some may call them "choices," indicating that they believe these to be only apparent, not real, manifestations of true agency. A more moderate view stipulates that choices are not expressions of free-floating freedom, but rather are forms of self-determination for which one can identify the kinds of pre-conditions that exist for all events. These might include the normal operation of behavioural or psychological laws; prior events or states of affairs affecting us (especially those that impinge on us personally); our upbringing and conditioning; and the social construction of experience and reality (our group-determined outlook on the world). If we were to trace our situational moment back far enough in time, or comprehend it in the widest context, such factors (which include our own previous choices) would be seen to be part of the way the natural world works, rather than as products of human freedom. So while our actions undeniably play a role in producing outcomes, and figure in the account we give of them, this fact does not by itself show that they are free.

One of the differences between fatalism and determinism, then, is that for fatalism, some, if not all events happen for reasons that cannot in principle be fathomed or enumerated and therefore remain beyond the reach of the intellect. Fatalists believe that somewhere, somehow, in the very nature of things, certain patterns or unique occurrences are fixed and unalterable. Determinists, by contrast, assert that ultimately there are no mysteries in the universe, merely cases of ignorance or limited knowledge. Everything is subject to explanation for the determinist, because it happens for reasons that are intelligible and can, for the most part, be either immediately known or at least ascertained. That is, what cannot be known at present is still allegedly knowable in principle – given enough time, ingenuity, and resources. This outlook is wedded to science and in particular to the optimistic promise of all-encompassing theories, laws, and predictive powers that can be mastered and applied across the range of experience. In addition, as one author puts it, if determinism is true, then "all of these [explanatory elements] would reside in the public domain and hence be transparent to inquiring reason."[45] In sum, causes – if known – make things predictable (foreseeable, expected, capable of being anticipated, likely, more or less certain, and so on). And while some people (for example, believers in omens) have supposed that what's fated is foreseeable, most believers in fate would argue that exactly the key thing about fate is its unfathomable randomness or arbitrariness and its *un*predictability.[46]

Now if determinism entails that whatever happens is due to prior causes, and if, as some argue, this implies that there is a closed chain of events going back to the beginning of the universe, then everything must be brought about by states of affairs in the very remote past.[47] But doesn't this mean that what causes our thoughts and behaviours in the present is elusive too (having originated in dim primordial times), and that our course through life is set and unalterable, just as much for determinists as it is for fatalists? Yes, but as explained above, there remain important differences between the two kinds of beliefs. Determinists think that if we could clearly see into the past, we would find rational explanations of all present events. Fatalists deny this. Determinists regard our choices as part of the causal chain of events. For a systematic fatalist (one who believes fate rules universally), our choices are only productive if fate allows them to be so. She may continue to argue that even if it makes sense to say that we freely choose a course of action, fate might always intervene, in one way or another, at some point after our choice is made.[48] It's a bit less clear for the fatalists, therefore, whether our choices can ever really be efficacious.

Yet a fatalist may take an unexpected tack here: The suggestion might be offered that we can come to terms with our fate or even celebrate it. This seems to make room for a certain scope of freedom or unfettered self-determination even within what had appeared to be an otherwise closed system. Determinists agree that we can reconcile ourselves to the circumstances of our lives, but insist that whether we have a mind to accept such a reconciliation also itself results from prior conditions that lie outside of our control. That is, we either are or are not born the kind of persons who can accept what life dishes out; we are optimists or pessimists even in the womb (or earlier still). Some theorists go on to assert that determinism, if pressed far enough, becomes a form of fatalism. Whether this is the case is best left for those philosophers to work out who have an interest in the intricacies of determinism.[49]

An additional difference between fatalism and determinism – a curious one – should be noted. According to some proponents of fatalism, as noted earlier, whoever or whatever controls a person's fate can possibly, in some instances, be appeased or placated or negotiated with, and hence that which could have befallen someone can or might also be forestalled or lessened in severity. The heavy hand of fate can be stayed, as it were (perhaps). From this perspective (which is by no means universal among fatalists), you might be better off as a fatalist than as a determinist, since scientific laws, though they may be revised or superseded as knowledge progresses, are not subject to personal appeals and influence. (This is what we mean when we say, for instance, that objects "obey the laws of nature.")

Reflections

It is an article of faith, widely shared among the scientific community, that we live in a deterministic universe.[50] Looking at things in this manner yields a certain model (or range of models) of how explanations should or must work. But a solid number of thinkers have discovered reasons not only to question the above characterization of scientific explanation itself,[51] but also to propose different patterns of explanation that appear to be more appropriate for a range of other contexts of inquiry, including history, the study of human behaviour, biology, literature, the arts more generally, as well as everyday life.[52] Some also argue that achieving understanding is not necessarily the same kind of process as being able to give an explanation.[53] What follows from all of this for our concerns in this book? Two things, really. The first is that accounts of what happens in our lives that include references to fate as a formative influence are clearly of another sort than those pursued by science (and other disciplines, for that matter). There is no reason, however, to infer that fate-loaded accounts are therefore less valid formulations. The second thing that follows is that the point of talking about fate at all and featuring it in such accounts is precisely to capture elements of meaning and significance – often momentous – that are otherwise lost. Thinking about fate does not necessarily provide answers or resolve questions; likewise, references to fate do not necessarily produce insight (although they often seem to). The purpose of invoking fate is primarily to help us better discern life's patterns, identify what matters most to us, and achieve solace and come to terms with the way the world is or has (fortuitously) turned out for us.

There are numerous occasions in life when it might seem appropriate to either resign ourselves to our fate and/or celebrate its working in our favour. But it may be that what we are reacting to is just a matter of luck or a chance occurrence. How can we tell the difference? What would constitute compelling grounds for invoking fate as an explanation of a significant event or series of events? We might be tempted to reply that fate is the unknown factor left over when all other explanatory manoeuvres have been exhausted and there seems to be no plausible alternative account remaining (see formula on page 34). This response, however, while aiming in the right direction, is a bit facile, superficial, and in need of refinement.

The notion of fate embraces both the given conditions of one's life and the serendipitous circumstances that arise during life which are out of one's control. Now many events that we attribute to luck or chance can, in principle at any rate, be causally explained. Others can be "retrodicted," that is, inferred to have been likely, in a backwards-looking way, given conditions that were present and operative at the time they occurred. But what cannot be rationalized is why lucky (or unlucky) or indeed any other kind of chance events happened to me, to you, or to any particular individual at all. As Gelven puts it, "The question 'why me?' cannot therefore be answered by any account that merely explains what or how things happen."[54] Thus, in addition to our being in existence to begin with, here and now, possessing such-and-such inherited conditions, many things that take place – unpredictable things surpassing explanation – seem to be aspects of life that are governed by fate. As a character in Jane Smiley's novel *A Thousand Acres* affirms, "'I always think that things have to happen the way they do happen, that there are so many inner and outer forces joining at every event that it becomes a kind of fate. I learned from Buddhism that there's beauty, and certainly a lot of peace, in accepting that.'"[55] The role of fate in mapping the gross features of life, but also in fine-tuning each individual's pathway through it, is accentuated by another figure appearing in Rachel Cusk's novel *The Bradshaw Variations*. Cusk captures her subject's mental state at the moment when she reflects on a previous "realisation that her fate was inscribed in the smallest particles of her being, inextricable; that she would always love and despair and struggle and succeed without knowing quite why she did. She thinks of the passion she experienced with Dieter, a passion of the cells, of the smallest particles."[56] In a collection of short stories, Joanne Harris comes to the same insight:

"every choice, every step of the journey, from crossing the road to boarding that fatal flight, is governed by probabilities of near-infinite elegance and complexity."[57] Many other creative writers testify to the manner in which even the most minute and heedless decisions can abruptly change the course of one's life. These authors, speaking through their fictional surrogates, express essential truths about how we piece together our view of the world, and about how fate fills the interstices of existence. The point that is missed by critics who are quick to dismiss fateful thinking is that although fate ultimately surpasses our understanding in various ways, it nevertheless functions importantly within our humanly limited attempts to formulate the meaning of life and decode the world around us. Causal explanations of events and of things that happen to ourselves and to others – supplemented by references to fortune, luck, or chance – may provide illumination sufficient for most purposes of inquiry, but they cannot fully replace fate in our total outlook.

In Brief …

"Fate," unless otherwise specified, will be taken to refer to those circumstances of existence that are given and unalterable, or that come into play in a generally unexpected, arbitrary, inexplicable manner, and possess at least a potentially momentous impact on our lives.

This chapter has looked at different notions of fate and has introduced the idea of fate as a feature of everyday existence. We have found that more moderate forms of fateful thinking are of greater interest and usefulness than extreme forms because they are truer to our lived experience. Belief in fate is life-changing, and accepting this idea is a reasonable, pragmatic direction to follow. Doing so, however, does not entail that we must also embrace *fatalism* in the full-blown sense, as a metaphysical theory about the nature of ultimate reality. Who I am, who you are, is a matter of when and where our births occur, our genetic endowment, a thousand and one contingent circumstances that shape a life, and again, of the time, place, and condition of our deaths. At the most basic level, these things are determinations of fate; they represent *life's universal or shared dimension*. When we unpack what is meant by this, we do not automatically need to assume that there's some being, thing, or power that calculates or randomly disperses outcomes, with benevolence or malice, but just that these points of reference simply are what they are: starting-points, in-between markers, and endpoints of existence. Such factors are mysterious, to be sure, even if the processes behind some – perhaps many of them – can be explained causally. Why they are as they are is something that will always evade our comprehension.

2

FATE'S GLOBAL REACH

Fate is a raging storm blowing over the Land.
– Sumerian proverb[1]

The Jews … had ever been wanderers – cast out, exiled and tossed upon a sea of fate, hopeful of a safe harbour.
– Neil Oliver[2]

History is already written for us. We will accept our fate when it comes.
– Haitham Rashid[3]

The Scheme of Things

The general question that occupied chapter 1 can be reframed as follows: when we think about fate, what exactly are we thinking about; what sort of outlook do we have in mind? Those who hold that there is no such thing as fate and that the notion lacks any coherence or explanatory significance would of course reply that we are thinking about nothing at all or concocting a spurious and imaginary concept. But references to fate are far too abundant in people's worldviews, ways of speaking, and written works across the ages to be dismissed this easily. A multicultural perspective is therefore valuable in framing a more balanced approach to the subject. For as we've seen already, fate is often posited to function as a powerful factor in the unfolding of events. And it is believed to operate at various scales, ranging from our being in existence at all, to the experiences that alter the course of our own lives, and even on to occurrences that have historical or cosmic significance.

If we understand by "fatalism" the doctrine that human lives are ruled by one or more inscrutable and almighty external forces, then such a viewpoint is as old as human thought about ultimate matters, whether appearing in the guise of mythology, religion, superstition, or philosophy. In fact it has been argued, correctly, that "The concept of *fatalism* has been central to the development of religious and philosophical thought."[4] This claim arises from an awareness that when contemplating the whole of things, in reference to the individual or the group to which one belongs, the focus of concern turns very quickly to the question of what or who causes and controls events and circumstances. And cultures, as much as those individuals who inhabit them, define themselves in relation to myths about their origins and projected destinies. Hence we might even think of fate as the glue that has held many civilizations together, and perhaps still does. Or we might think of it as some kind of an essential bridge between mythology and life. To understand this better, we need to appreciate how fate entered into the thought systems and practices of our ancient ancestors.

The Conditions of Life

The systematic study of ideas shows that their emergence and development depends to a great extent on historical circumstances. And in the case of fate, this consideration points our attention to the living situations and survival struggles and strategies of bygone eras. We know that human life on the planet, past and present, confronts a wide variety of perennial challenges, and responds with relative degrees of success. In some respects, early human groups existed especially precariously as they experimented not only with living arrangements but also with methods of understanding and managing the world around them. They faced many major problems: harsh climates; periodic, unpredictable floods, or else droughts and crop failures in some regions; environmental depletion; unavailability of needed materials; insect swarms, devastating famines, plagues, and epidemics; autocratic rulers and violent power struggles, as well as threats of invasion – plus actual invasions, plundering, and cultural destruction and assimilation. Mesopotamia (including Sumer, Akkad, Assyria, and Babylon) provides one example.

A very early cradle of civilization, Mesopotamia lay between the Tigris and Euphrates Rivers in what is now largely Iraq. Neolithic settlements in the region date to 10,000 BCE, and written records go back to about 3,100 BCE. These and other sorts of archaeological evidence reveal a very sophisticated and ingenious people whose achievements include elaborate artworks and architecture and establishment of the first cities, as well as the invention of the wheel, cursive script, mathematics, astronomy, maps, and the world's first work of literature (the *Epic of Gilgamesh*). Although Mesopotamia was a fertile region, daily life in a place of harsh temperatures required hard work, and low-lying marshy flatlands made for frequent, unpredictable, and destructive flooding by the major rivers, as well as offering opportunities for invasion and conquest. Living at the mercy of mighty rivers is a dominant theme of both past and present societies, and it is well captured by archaeologist and historian Neil Oliver's dramatically stripped-down characterization of Egypt in the time of the pharaohs: "The fates of all, from highest to lowest, depended on the Nile."[5]

In the ancient world, class membership and social status were often strictly defined and reinforced. Servitude and extremely demanding physical labour was the only way of life for most. Cruelty was commonly practiced upon vanquished foreigners as well as on group members who transgressed against the social order or the accepted belief system. Retribution and ceremonial killings were commonplace. The Royal Standard of Ur, a Sumerian war panel (c. 2,600–2,400 BCE), depicts the king's army brutally crushing hapless bloodied and dying enemies with their horses and chariots, while elsewhere it represents bound and naked prisoners awaiting the king's decision on their ultimate lot. The Roman Empire was steeped in bloodshed and sacrifice, most famously in the Colosseum. To take just one other instance, Vestal Virgins, responsible for maintaining the eternal sacred fire of Rome, were buried alive if found to be unchaste. Mesoamerican Mayan culture, from about 250 CE to the seventeenth century, required the performance of ritual human sacrifice and related atrocious deeds in order to honour and appease the gods, dedicate buildings, and install new rulers. Given such practices of early cultures, it's little wonder that deities were conceived as authoritarian, angry, punishing, harsh, and relentless – or that an inscrutable, towering force of fate, whose blows might just as likely be acts of reprisal or of randomness, had to be reckoned with. Both oppressors and the oppressed could rationalize their position in the scheme of things by belief in a world order ordained by fate or a similar force.

At the same time, fate served as an explanation for events – an appeal of last resort, perhaps, but an explanation nonetheless. Explanations often have the character of reducing the unfamiliar to the familiar, as when we come to realize that some phenomenon that puzzles us belongs to a type we already know and understand. For instance, a liquid that tastes sour, like an acid, is discovered to actually be an acid; the spectrum of light given off by a distant planet is compared to Earth's and then analyzed; a wartime general's strategy is based upon the best information available as well as familiarity with similar situations in the past. But explanations don't always conform to this pattern; and in everyday life, as in science, we may feel required to invoke unfamiliar principles or entities. Scientific explanation routinely calls upon such resources as space-time relativity, quantum mechanics, black holes, bubble universes, hitherto unknown properties of materials, and counterintuitive conceptual inventions of all kinds. (One seemingly fanciful scenario concerning the fate of the universe, for instance, features "spacetime decay" caused by "an expanding bubble of nothing."[6]) People in their everyday lives do their best to grasp the world and their place in it, and for better or worse this may end up including explanation by reference to fate. Proponents of causal explanation may insist that once a causal account of an occurrence is given, there's nothing left to explain. In some instances, however, that stance might be dogmatic and shortsighted. For it may turn out that a "complete" account of a particular phenomenon (if there is such a thing) needs to adopt a different pattern. This could be expressed as follows:

EXPLANATION = CAUSALITY (LAWS + CONDITIONS PREVAILING AT THE TIME) + CHANCE CIRCUMSTANCES + FATE,

where fate is the X-factor that remains when more familiar and experientially verifiable ingredients have been exhausted and are seen to have fallen short of providing the degree of insight being sought.

A Road Well Travelled (I)

The ubiquity of belief in fate and fateful ideas is something to marvel at. The topic of fate brings us into contact with primal cosmologies and the most basic human emotions, such as fear, anxiety, and joy. In studying fate, then, we immerse ourselves in the very familiar territory within which we must negotiate much of our existence: the unknown, hope, uncertainty, triumph, despair, and surprise. In what follows, the global reach of fate and fateful ideas will be examined.

Any overview of the role fate has played or plays in different cultures runs up against the problem that there is no single concept or approach that adequately captures all renderings of fate's operation in human life. As already noted, fate is often seen as an autonomous force, one that either serves the purposes of divinities, or is an aspect of their power. But fate can also be cast as an independent, even superior agency (that may have the final word over how things turn out, or, on the other hand, may be appealed to or bargained with).[7] Astrology, ancient forms of divination, casting of lots, consulting the *I Ching* or the prophesies of Nostradamus (1503–1566), as well as more "modern" innovations, such as tarot cards and ouija boards, provide examples of practices that demonstrate the independence of fate from any particular religious framework or theistic will.

By contrast, in early Greece "the Fates" or "the goddesses of fate" were among the universally accepted allies or respected colleagues of the gods. In Hesiod's *Theogony* (eighth century BCE), these figures first appear as fatherless "daughters of the Night [Nyx]," but are later said by him to be the progeny of Zeus and Themis. The Fates (also known as the Moirai) are three spinsters named Clotho, Lachesis, and Atropos. Clotho spins the thread of life, Lachesis assigns each human a portion of thread at birth, and Atropos carries out the act of cutting the thread at death. It is interesting to note that these functions of fate all have to do with time, specifically the allotment of a person's lifetime (one's fate being conceived of as one's "share" or "portion"). (Similar ideas are found in the Islamic belief-system: see page 92.) Other aspects of fate – its various incursions into our lives – are not assigned agency in this picture.

The spinning or weaving metaphor that connects the responsibilities of these three sister-goddesses reappears in many other traditions and guises. Worth citing in this connection is the "widely spread Semitic myth of a goddess of Fate," a personage who appears in Babylonian mythology as Ishtar and who is identified with the planet Venus. She "spins the cord of life" which is severed by another goddess, Bau.[8] In Norse mythology, the Valkyries are female figures charged with deciding who lives and who perishes in battle; and the Norns, likewise female beings, control the fate of both humans and gods. They are: Urd, Verdandi, and Skuld, who represent past, present, and future respectively. The Norns dwell by Yggdrasil, the central tree of the cosmos, and they weave the thread of each entity's destiny. This spinning motif is probably why we use expressions like "weaving a life," "the web of life," "the fabric of life," or "the warp and weft of life." As one scholar points out, while the symbols of weaving are usually associated with "processes of creation and growth," they also convey "negative connotations as instruments of binding or tools of entrapment."[9]

This imagery of weaving functions as part of a much larger context by means of which humans have situated themselves within the totality of the universe. Giulia Piccaluga, scholar of classics and religion, explains that "the conception of creation as a whole – both the cosmic order and man's place within it – as the product of some type of binding activity, whether of knotting, tying, twining, or weaving, is quite widespread." She adds that cross-cultural practices of knot-making accordingly possess a long history of empowerment: "knots are used to control a reality that is itself abstract, fluctuating, evanescent. Guilt, time, or fate itself, by being concretized in a knot, comes under the control of the person who ties it and who thereby resolves a given situation."[10] Fate and allied concepts thus enter into regular, culture-defining rituals and other activities and images that are relied upon to give stability to everyday life. We also speak of finishing important business as "tying things up" or "tying up loose ends," and of marriage as "tying the knot." The expressions "yarning," "spinning a yarn," or "telling a good yarn" convey in a more informal manner the act of bringing things together in a story (which is not necessarily true but nevertheless builds the bonds of community).[11]

The Greeks thought of fate (*Moira*) in a more depersonalized, abstract way too, as a principle of necessity or inevitability embedded within the nature of reality. This conception is present in the works of Homer (eighth century BCE), who "speaks in several places of one single Moira, whose decisions are irrevocable and to whom even the gods are subjected."[12] In this manifestation, fate has been characterized as a "pattern of doom" that "exhibited no purpose and no transcendence; it just was."[13] A different interpretation is suggested by Jakob Larsen and P.J. Rhodes when they note that the Greeks' "sense of [moral] order extended to the entire cosmos whose proper running was guaranteed by fate, generally with the gods' co-operation."[14] The Greeks, who were irrepressible storytellers, perhaps more often than not had an account of things that rationalized the operations of fate as payback for wrongdoing or as the teaching of a harsh but necessary lesson (see, for example, the story of Antigone, page 110).

This Greek tradition shaped the thought of Socrates (c. 470–399 BCE), one of the most important figures in the history of Western philosophy, who serves as a kind of exemplar for coming to terms with one's lot in life. Socrates does not fear death, believing that the soul is a prisoner in the body, from which it seeks release into a happier, more profound afterlife. It's just as well that he believed this, for Socrates becomes condemned to death by the Athenian state for "impious teachings" about the established religion of his day. If we are to credit the account of his disciple and student Plato (c. 428–347 BCE), we have a historically accurate picture of Socrates "cheerfully accepting his fate."[15] Some people may willingly accept their fate, others grudgingly, still others not at all. Some among these may be active, self-determining individuals, and some may be mere passive spectators of their own lives. But regardless of where we fall on this spectrum we generally speak of accepting fate only when the future for someone (or for ourselves) is decided by others or by external circumstances and there is little we can do about the situation other than await the outcome. Thus Socrates was perhaps the kind of person who didn't even need to "steel himself to his fate." Often people do, however, and this process becomes a test of what they are made of. We will encounter many examples of this transformative resolve in chapter 6.

The ancient Romans venerated those figures known as Sibyls, or female seers, and Sibylline oracles were passed down in written form and held in adulation by medieval Church Fathers. As folklore scholar Ronald Grambo observes, the Sibyls themselves "became in the Middle Ages equivalent to the prophets of the Old Testament."[16] Rome's Stoic philosophers (third century BCE-second century CE) held that fate rules the universe and for this reason, those who wish to live the best life should engage themselves appropriately with the world around them, accepting that "we are merely actors in a play written by someone else ... But regardless of the role we are assigned, we must play it to the best of our ability ... We must learn to adapt ourselves to the environment into which fate has placed us and do our best to love the people with whom fate has surrounded us. We must learn to welcome whatever falls to our lot and persuade ourselves that whatever happens to us is for the best."[17] The lesson here is simple: "Do not struggle against the inevitable or against providence; go with it, and make the best of it. Change what you are able to and accept the rest as it presents itself." Today someone who is identified as "stoic" is regarded as taking whatever comes his way resolutely and without complaint. Such an individual, in the popular imagination, is the model of "being fatalistic" about life. The Stoics' notion of fate provides an insight into the reason why in Rome a slave (Epictetus, 55–135 CE) and an emperor (Marcus Aurelius, 121–180 CE) could both live according to the same philosophical creed. But it is obvious as well that a view of this type readily lends itself to reinforcing a social order that privileges some over others, together with its prevailing power structure. In that respect it serves as part of the imperial ideology of that ancient era.

Is there a paradox involved in asserting, on the one hand, that one's position in life is fixed and, on the other, that she should grab hold of the personal fate assigned to her and "go with it"? A big question arises here, one that interpreters of Stoicism have wrestled with for a long time. John Sellars argues that for the Stoics, "fate works *through* us. We are ourselves *contributors* to fate and parts of the larger natural world governed by it."[18] So according to this view, the path of fulfilment in life is to acknowledge an order of things which we have no power to alter, and to develop ourselves as best we're able in relation to it. Kai Whiting and Leonidas Konstantakos interpret this idea a bit more powerfully, by means of the observation that "character is the only guarantee you have of succeeding in life, and ... strength of character matters most when the odds are stacked against you."[19] Fate challenges us to excel, then, and to take up the mantle of courageous self-assertion. (We will revisit this theme in subsequent chapters, and especially in chapter 6.)

A Road Well Travelled (II)

The breadth of fate-centred perspectives is on display in a number of important scholarly works. A landmark conference on "fatalistic beliefs," held a few decades ago, covers the entire waterfront and abundantly illustrates this wealth of ideas. Presenters locate fatalistic beliefs in sources as diverse as Greek tragedies, Finnish proverbs, Icelandic sagas, poems from pre-Islamic Arabia (including Babylon), Islamic texts, east European folk narratives, texts from ancient Egypt's Eighteenth Dynasty (the period of pharaoh Tutankhamun, Queen Nefertiti, and other luminaries), Teutonic, Old Norse, and Old English literature, the religion of the Lepcha people residing in Sikkim state (Northeast India), and the belief-system of Bantu tribes who inhabit Africa's Great Lakes region. In addition, the conference considers oracular practices of ancient China in the Shang-Yin Dynasty – over a millennium BCE.[20] History of religion specialist and conference participant Kees Bolle designates fate as a "travelling idea," which took hold as the influence of Greek thinkers spread across the ancient world and converged with other traditions.[21] Such historical developments, as he observes, enabled the notion of fate to blossom forth among widely separated and diverse cultures. We often think of artifacts and inventions, cuisine, clothing, traditions, and the like as migrating via exploration and conquest, and tend to overlook ideas. But ideas are equally peripatetic and often even more potently influential.

Other compendiums illustrate the universality of fate equally well. In a massive twentieth-century encyclopedic work titled *The Mythology of All Races*, one researcher states that "This idea of a Fate bound up with the heavens is common to all the Turk-related peoples …

Each [individual] has been given a special ruler of fate, which follows him faithfully from the moment of birth. The Mongols call this spirit, which does not desert man as long as he is in favour with the heavens, Dzol ('happiness') Dzagagatši."[22] Here we encounter not only the notion of a ruling fate – a kind of invisible, mysterious hand operating behind the scene, that is widespread among certain cultural groups – but also the variation that everyone has a personal fate-guardian who looks after their welfare. (This concept is also present in Norse mythology.) "Another early concept," we learn elsewhere, "describes the sky as a huge tree overshadowing the earth, the stars being the fruits or leaves which hang from its branches … This thought … which is found among so many nations, also underlies the idea of the tree of life … The tree of fate, whose leaves or fruits symbolize events or the lives of men, represents the same thought: the past as well as the future is written in the stars."[23] Fate encompasses everything that exists, everything that we do. In this conception, we are literally made of fate, inasmuch as it is the tree of life, on whose fruit we subsist. Similarly, we learn in the *Encyclopedia of World Cultures* that the Vlachs – a Balkan Eastern Orthodox ethnic group with scattered presence and diasporas in Romania, North America, Australia, and elsewhere – are said to have a belief system in which "Everything related to human beings and existence usually is attributed to fate."[24]

The theme of fate is also said to be a defining feature of Persian literature generally (meaning the traditions of Iran and Afghanistan). As Ronald Johnson reports, "A popular religious or philosophical theme that is expressed in Persian literature is *qesmet*, or fate. Persians believe that all unexplained occurrences are the will of God, and that most things in life are controlled by fate rather than by humans. The unpredictable nature of life is sometimes used to justify the pursuit of pleasure."[25] Abd-al-Hosayn Zarrinkub describes this all-encompassing matrix of fate in greater detail: "human destiny is pre-determined and whatever happens in the world follows a pre-ordained course which cannot be altered except by the will of God

… This belief, couched in a variety of ways, is reflected in many aspects of Persian culture including literature, mystical writings, folklore, and popular expressions. The reliance on auguries, religious vows and pledges and supplicatory gifts, can be regarded as strategies for ameliorating the inherent harshness of such beliefs and the paralysing effect they can inflict on human endeavour, making any effort or struggle appear futile and worthless."[26] From these descriptions, some may jump to the conclusion that belief in fate is merely a product of ignorance and craven negativity. But a more insightful approach would be to affirm that the humility and supplication engendered by belief in fate respect and respond proportionally to the limitations of human knowledge and power to control things.

Belief systems that anthropologists describe as "totemic" connect humans to natural and spiritual orders that predetermine and prescribe our very essence and identity. As one source suggests, "Totemism's importance lies in providing individuals and groups with direct and life-sustaining links back to the very beginnings of society itself."[27] But such visions simultaneously project notions of inviolable rules and rituals. Australian Indigenous peoples' "Dreamtime," for example, is an outlook embracing many ancestral myths of creation and setting forth modes of obligatory conduct. Those who live in accordance with it certainly have a guiding destiny; but it is also arguable that there is an element of fate in any system that includes laws governing behaviour that themselves emanate from an omnipotent spiritual realm.

Philosopher Hartley Burr Alexander, writing about North American First Nations' worldviews, maintains that "there is hardly a tribe that does not possess its belief in what may very properly be called a Great Spirit, or Great Mystery, or Master of Life."[28] In the case of the Omaha tribe of the Great Plains (Siouan), this is Wakonda, and according to a detailed study of the Omaha people's traditional cosmology, co-authored by anthropologist Alice C. Fletcher and tribe member Francis La Flesche, "All experiences in life were believed to be directed by Wakonda, a belief that gave rise to a kind of fatalism. In the face of calamity, the thought, 'This is ordered by Wakonda,' put a stop to any form of rebellion against the trouble and often to any effort to overcome it." Their account also records that whereas men used a prayer pipe to connect with Wakonda, "generally [a] sorrowful or burdened woman simply called on the mysterious power she believed to have control of all things, to know all desires, all needs, and able to send the required help."[29] This is another example, emanating from a different and unique cultural context, of the ancient tendency to derive a certain kind of solace and a steadfast yet calm attitude from belief in fate. Interestingly, we saw this same attitude earlier as a defining feature of Stoicism.

Very remote in time and place from this tribal belief-system, we find Brian Fallon's engaging description of life in twentieth-century rural Ireland: "In a country town, everybody knows you and your family, or at least knows about you; every death or birth is a kind of communal event, and there is a certain sense of an enveloping cocoon of fatalism, of a preordained round ending in the local churchyard. It is a difficult thing to put into words, but it is felt by everyone and permeates the small, tight world; and though the town itself may be left behind, you are marked in certain ways for life."[30] The "enveloping cocoon of fatalism," so well described here, might be thought of as incredibly stultifying, but it is turned by Fallon into a mysterious and universal comfort-dimension of life, with which most people can empathize. Fate has its less attractive, foreboding aspect, yet strangely enough it also reverberates with the dynamics of togetherness and existential security.

A final example of fate's omnipresence in human life spotlights Austrian composer Gustav Mahler (1860–1911), who is widely acclaimed for his many groundbreaking orchestral works. In his Sixth Symphony (which premiered in 1906), Mahler calls for the percussion strokes of a gigantic, purpose-built hammer, widely believed to represent the "blows of fate" that can decisively alter the direction of a life, or even end it.[31] Mahler thus gives symbolic and highly audible musical form to the fateful circumstances everyone experiences in one way or another.

Fate's Action at a Distance

We saw earlier that fate has been characterized as a "travelling idea." It is not, of course, in any way unique in that respect. But it is informative to view ideas from this perspective because it suggests both the progressive enlargement of their range of influence on people's thinking and the remoteness of causation that can be identified in some manner as fateful. How can we best understand this? Historian Peter Frankopan offers a fascinating insight into the theme of fate as a controlling force, energized by those unknown to us in distant places who are inadvertent history-makers. Seventeenth- and eighteenth-century battles for ascendancy among regional powers such as England, France, and Austria had a determining effect on events in remote colonies. Tracing this line of development, Frankopan shrewdly observes that, among other things, "It was also becoming clear that what happened in Europe could determine one's fate on the other side of the world."[32] One may justifiably feel that the same dynamic has only become exacerbated over the centuries since then. World history has become local history to a large extent (and vice-versa), as many examples can attest (such as terrorist acts, international sports events, the invention of new technology, or the escape of pathogens from a foreign laboratory). Remote planning by total strangers can effectively seal the fate of many ordinary, innocent people living in faraway locations (for instance, the decisions of wealthy dictators, world monetary fund managers, trade negotiators, and stockbrokers).

A further case of remote determinations of fate worth examining in detail is provided by the atomic bombings of Japan during the final stage of the Second World War. The crucial decision to use the ultimate weapon was made half a world away in Washington, DC (by President Harry S. Truman, 1884–1972), and the precise drop locations were selected by a joint US scientific-military targets committee meeting in the weapons research headquarters at Los Alamos, New Mexico. It is well known that the second atom bomb was dropped on the city of Nagasaki on 9 August 1945, three days after the first one annihilated Hiroshima. Virtually unknown, however, are a few background facts. To begin with, the secondary target until early in August had been Kyoto, but this plan was eventually scrapped because of the ancient city's cultural importance. The city of Kokura then took Kyoto's place as the target and the bomb was lined up to be delivered there on the eleventh. The bomb-drop date was then moved back two days from the eleventh because of bad weather predictions for that day. Poor weather and lingering atmospheric smoke from the Allies' firebombing of other Japanese cities presented problems on the new date as well, and so, after three unsuccessful bombing runs over Kokura, with the loaded aircraft running low on fuel, Nagasaki (the next city on the list, where the weather happened briefly to be clear) got selected, and the rest is history.

Fateful impacts are felt not only across space, but also across time. In *The River Capture*, Mary Costello depicts an episode in the life of her protagonist Luke, who has innocently stumbled into a difficult, complex, and troubled relationship clouded by repercussions flowing from others' acts performed decades in the past. In no way could this influence have been predicted. Luke's situation causes him to reflect "On how the hands of fate can reach across fifty years and stick a knife in him and her and her and her."[33] Those who have discovered later in life previously hidden, major facts about their backgrounds would certainly understand this effect all too easily. Beyond such dramatic events, we all experience daily the effects of many factors beyond our control, such as war mongering, climate change, pollution, contested energy supplies, and the decisions of political leaders who aren't listening to those whom they are meant to serve.

On a different, but related level of analysis, it can be observed that many external factors help to promote and give new roots to ideas as they spread across the globe. Reflecting on the astonishing variety of beliefs in fate that present themselves for our examination, Grambo recommends the following perspective: "One should always take into account the possibility that belief in fate … has been formed and modified not only by ecological, political, social, economic factors, but also by movements of population and by the fact that belief systems in general … can be spread and transmitted both orally and by literary means … There are always factors which develop and promote the existence of certain belief systems, certain attitudes, norms, values … The interesting fact is that belief in fate has been institutionalized."[34] This way of looking at fate opens up new vistas (still largely unexplored) to historians and sociologists. Seeing it as a defining aspect of a particular culture, way of life, or belief system is productive not only of a deeper understanding of fate, but also of the diverse arrangements by which human life has been organized.

On Fatalism and Organized Religion

One of the most significant ways in which people's outlooks have been shaped is through religion. Over time, monotheistic religion has taken hold in the minds of many people as the "correct" kind of belief system. Such a stance leads periodically to wars and terrorist acts initiated by those who think their particular variety or sect of monotheism needs to be imposed on "infidels," "heretics," or "unbelievers," wherever they are to be found. Those who adhere to the major monotheistic religions (Judaism, Christianity, and Islam) often attribute good or bad consequences to God's will, claiming that "God is on our side," and petitioning God to intervene in the temporal order so as to bring about some favoured result. But arguably, these viewpoints and entreaties place God in the role of an incomprehensible, overriding capacity that in the end seems almost indistinguishable from fate. One might go a step further to assert that fate is a paradigm for omnipotent deities of all sorts, who are inscrutable, remote, and generally unappeasable. Even the "special-interest" gods of Greek, Roman, and Hindu pantheons fall into the same pattern, having insurmountable power in their own realms.

The historical evolution of religion is more complicated still. As some scholars have argued, a clash between monotheistic religion – particularly Christianity – and belief in fate was entirely to be expected. The reasons are not difficult to fathom. Fatalism, if it coexists with a religious perspective, generally must leave room in the universe for an independent force or counterforce. Monotheism, on the other hand (by definition) features a single, all-powerful deity, and consequently, monotheistic religions must exclude the idea of fate as a separate agency, operating on its own and possibly capable of overruling the will of deities, which had been a commonplace belief in earlier cultures. In short, monotheism can internalize fatalism but cannot leave it to fly solo.

In addition, Christianity promotes ideals of freedom, self-determination, and personal accountability for one's actions, whereas belief in fate imposes important limits on all of these. Essayist Margaret Visser states that in contrast to earlier views of the universe, Christianity, with its Jewish heritage, "replaces time as cyclic and eternal recurrence (time as fate) with emergent possibility: change, discovery, hope, and liberation … It insisted from the beginning that an individual was … a free being of intrinsic worth and unfathomable depth, living in relationship with others while creatively engaged in the ongoing project that is his or her own life."[35] This is the more positive message of Christianity, to be sure. Yet it seems to be in constant danger of being devoured by the fundamental contradiction lying at its heart: that God is the all-powerful, all-knowing, all-good creator of everything, who – fatefully – foresees all that is or ever will be. For this reason, important Christian voices developed quite influential fatalistic strands of thought. And fatalistic tendencies can be identified within Judaism as well. We will consider these forms of belief further in chapters 4 and 5.

In Brief …

As we have seen, many people (whether or not they are religious in the generally accepted sense) believe or have believed in fate, including members of some very strong and vibrant cultures. Reflecting on the wide array of outlooks such as those discussed in this chapter has led some to suggest that belief in fate and fatalism resulted from unenlightened perspectives on life prevailing within early pagan, polytheistic cultures. In this spirit, fatalism has, for example, been labeled as an "appallingly primitive prescientific doctrine."[36] Unfortunate and inaccurate caricatures such as this, however, spring from misunderstanding as well as from the cultural chauvinism, snobbishness, and desire for superiority characteristic of the present age. No doubt specific factors are evident in certain eras that make fatalistic beliefs loom larger in the shared consciousness of humanity. People have often felt that they live in dangerous, volatile, unpredictable times. At those intervals, they might be more likely to fall back upon ideas that ease the burden of understanding, if only by reassuring them that there *are* forces in control of the world that ensure some sense of orderliness exists beneath the chaotic surface of everyday events. Even if fate is beyond appeal, beliefs about it may yield warning signs of what is impending. But beyond all this, it remains the case that fate and fatalism are human constants, that is, guideposts for existential orientation and the conduct of everyday life that continually reassert themselves through a variety of historical circumstances. Probably the most we could say by way of summary is that to a large extent, cultures have shifted over time from those in which fate was deemed to be the central component of life to those in which it is weighed as just one explanatory factor among many.

3

THE LANGUAGE OF FATE

I am afraid we are little better than straws upon the water; we may flatter ourselves that we swim, when the current carries us along.
– Lady Mary Wortley Montague[1]

Whistle at sea and you are as good as done for, whether you believe in God or fate, it makes no difference.
– Roy Jacobsen[2]

Expressions, Judgments, Insights (I)

Fate is not just a punchy four-letter F-word. We have already uncovered the fact that it is a robust and multifaceted notion with deep meanings and complex origins. And judging from the number and variety of expressions centering on or related to it, one might reasonably suppose that people quite often structure their lives and thoughts with reference to fate. Certainly, we talk about it and allude to it with great frequency.

There are ways of speaking that indicate that an element of fate stalks our everyday existence: "a twist of fate," "a quirk of fate," "a brush with fate," "in fate's grasp," "written in the stars," "as fate would have it," "tempting fate," "what fate decreed," "leaving the outcome to fate." When we say that people are being "abandoned to their fate," we mean to underline a condition of extreme vulnerability – that nothing can be done to avert a certain development or an unknown calamity. And some things do seem to happen with ironclad necessity. In *The Scapegoat*, a novel by Daphne du Maurier (1907–1989), for example, the main character meets his identical double by accident and, under peculiar circumstances, they swap lives, each taking up where the other left off. At the outset, he muses, "it seemed to me that what was happening was fated, inevitable, that I should never be rid of him or he of me: he would follow me downstairs and come with me in the car, and I should never shake him off. He was my shadow or I was his, and we were bound to each other through eternity."[3] This chance meeting, in his view, was a "freak of fortune." Many of our life experiences have a similar, though probably less dramatic profile. Chance contacts that lead to a great new job opportunity; meeting one's lifetime partner; getting into some life-changing altercation over a trivial incident – these all may strike us as having an aspect of inevitability about them. Whenever we see our personal existence as unfolding within a universal scheme of things, we may have the same kind of perception. This is not a matter of inflating our own importance, however, but rather the reverse: of seeing human agency as limited and contingent. This perception of limited agency is underlined by the way in which we often speak of outcomes in the natural world. For example: "It was years before Sally learned the fate of her father." Here, fate is equivalent to just what happened or what became of someone.

References to fate may simply spotlight decisions other people, perhaps those in positions of authority, make for us. Or they may single out situations in which a particular possible outcome cannot be predicted, but its impact, should it occur, is well known (for example, contracting a certain disease or facing bankruptcy). A photograph on the Internet shows refugees "awaiting their fate" in a certain country. A newspaper story describes someone who wonders whether he'll "share the same fate as his brother." A personal narrative breaks off with the sentence "At that point fate intervened." Observations of the following kind are also very common: "Fate seems to be the only explanation of this event" or "She narrowly avoided meeting a similar fate" or "How was he to know that he'd made a fatal mistake in choosing the captain's company?" Anthony Doerr's powerful novel *About Grace* features a character who has fateful premonitions in dreams, but narrowly succeeds in evading what they foretell. Yet in one hospital scene, he is said to have "trod softly … past the closed doors behind which people waited in the grips of their various fates."[4] Thus, even the gift of being able to remain beyond fate's long reach is something not to be disturbed; one can't pass it on to others or take it for granted in oneself. The reference to doors in the preceding example is interesting, because we also characterize the intrusion of a sinister force in our lives as the moment when "fate comes knocking on the door."

Some phrases that allude to the workings of fate are more elliptical. Life teaches us about "what's written in the stars," "the way the cookie crumbles," what "was meant to happen," or "following the path marked out for me." A few expressions manage to be both elliptical and utterly blunt at the same time, such as "shit (or stuff) happens." From some doleful perspectives, these last observations seem to pretty well cover all of life's events. And often, somewhere within the range of events that happen, lurks "a fate worse than death" – for example, social ostracism, a life of slavery, or becoming severely handicapped. All of the above sayings imply that fateful intervention by the universe is an ever-present possibility and that the course of events cannot be relied upon to follow a probable, expected, accustomed, welcome, or for that matter even unwelcome pattern. There are among us, however, individuals who apparently achieve success in "cheating fate" or "casting fate to the wind," and their stories cannot help but intrigue us. So too do the stories of those who seem fated to fall short of their ambitions. In these cases, reflection on fate is used as a yardstick for measuring what has been felt as attained or not attained at a certain point in life's ongoing story.

References to fate often point to the impending outcome of a process that is already underway: "His fate hangs in the balance"; "She faces several possible fates of equal gravity"; "The outcome rests in the lap of fate." People generally seem to be open to the possibility that an unknown factor may take over events or circumstances, for better or worse, at any time. We all know that life is a precarious adventure, a risky game. It doesn't take much to tip the balance for or against success in achieving our goals, in being happy or sad, healthy or unhealthy, getting into an accident or avoiding one, and so on. And it's this good or bad or mixed fortune, this unpredictable element, that ushers in the idea of fate as an ever-present, potentially destabilizing influence. Jonathan Schell's bestselling 1982 book *The Fate of the Earth* made an effective appeal to this sensibility in its title. In the book Schell explains in great detail how nuclear war would cause a massive release of smoke, dust, and debris and, eventually, a universal deep freeze known as "nuclear winter" that would destroy almost all life on our planet.[5] Certainly, from the human standpoint, this would be the dreaded apocalypse.

Many of the examples we've considered underscore the "chancy" aspect of fate – that anyone's fate might have been different, indeed a whole lot different, if it weren't for entirely contingent factors surrounding their time and place in existence. Being in the midst of a nuclear war needs no further elaboration to serve as an example. But even at a much more mundane level the point still stands. Thus, as journalist Jonathan Freedland observes, with reference to refugees and displaced migrants across the world, "but for the lottery of fate, it would not be them on those boats – it would be us."[6] This is the kind of realization that brings fate, luck, chance, fortune, and destiny into a convergent whole.

Expressions, Judgments, Insights (II)

A word that has crept into English over time, signifying the incursion of fate into someone's life situation, is *kismet*, which we met in chapter 2 as *qesmet*. This word springs from similar roots in Turkish, Urdu, Hindi, Persian, and Arabic, the Arabic *qisma*, meaning division, portion, or lot, and deriving from *qasama* ("to divide"). *Kismet* has been appropriated by the Western world to express its own fascination with fate. A celebrated 1953 musical called *Kismet* played on Broadway and on London's West End, with a film version following; but about a dozen other film and stage shows have used the same title, as well as many other cultural products.[7] The actor Aristotelis ("Telly") Savalas (1922–1994) starred as the bald, lollipop-sucking, sunglasses-wearing Lt Theo Kojak in the eponymous 1970s TV crime drama series and, on catching the bad guy, would wryly comment, "*Kismet*, baby!"

Then there are expressions that capture the seriousness of fate's intervention. Something that's been done may "seal one's fate," or lead to "the fateful or inexorable consequence" one dreads (see discussion of the self-fulfilling prophecy in chapter 4). But all is not gloom and doom either, because you may become "master of your fate," "gain control of your fate," or "triumph by the hand of fate" – or so it may seem on the surface of things or in the short term.

Objects may meet their fates as well. There are various kinds of examples that illustrate how we speak about such occurrences. An article in *National Geographic* magazine proclaims: "Newfound tiny planet may be a glimpse of Earth's ultimate fate."[8] Here, "Earth's ultimate fate" concerns the demise of our planet in accordance with a causal process that scientists can fully understand and pretty well predict. On the other hand, sometimes an object's fate depends on human behaviour or intervention: "She determined the fate of her favourite hairbrush when she hurled it, in a fit of rage, against the stone wall of the kitchen"; "The fate of Mom's jewellery remains unknown to this day, but it pretty clearly disappeared when her memory started to fail." We see in these examples that the fate of a thing is often the product of human choice or impulse, although the exact outcome may not be completely up to the agent concerned. There are also cases where a thing's ultimate fate seems to be mostly a function of the slow and relentless way in which nature operates. For instance: "The fate of his expensive toolbox was to be left out in the torrential rain that night, which pretty well ruined its contents." Misfortunes may of course revisit a person: "Years later, his stamp collection suffered the same fate." Fateful observations of this type, about what befalls ordinary things or cherished personal property, are quite regularly made. And not infrequently, objects get their revenge as they assume a more active agency: "His fate was determined by the detour sign, which had been blown around by the wind to point in the wrong direction."

People speak fairly routinely of an individual's (or their own) "lot in life." This is an interesting take on fate because it again raises the issue of justice and injustice in the universe, considered earlier in chapter 1. Most of us would like to think that good conduct, kindness, generosity, and so on are rewarded, while bad or evil behaviour is punished. Essentially, this means that the law of *karma* really does work as it's supposed to; that some moral principle operates in the world to assure people get their just deserts. Yet references to one's lot in life seem to negate that hope. You don't necessarily "get what's coming to you" (good or bad), but only what the universe arbitrarily dispenses. Perhaps, too, we may think that we are occasionally rescued from poor outcomes by mysterious acts of divine interposition: "There, but for the grace of God go I"; "It was a miracle that I lived through that." Much of the energy that has fuelled and sustained religious doctrines of justice, punishment, and the afterlife as a place of ultimate retribution and reward comes from disgruntlement over the apparent or actual lack of fairness that prevails in human life. That these doctrines tie in with a fateful view of the cosmos is especially revealing, given that organized religion, by many accounts, supposedly supersedes the allegedly cruder, more "primitive" belief in fate.

Interior Monologues and Conversations

If we are persuaded that fate is in the hands of God or Allah or any other supreme deity, then all we can do is guess how to act in life in order to increase the probability of the best outcome for ourselves. We can't say, "I'm doing this in order to ensure the optimum outcome," because within this belief-structure no one possesses the power to guarantee *any* particular outcome for any particular person or persons, including themselves. The best we can do is "play the hand that we are dealt" and cling to hope for the future.

People spend much time pondering the human condition, and for some this is a lifetime preoccupation. A good deal of this fascination and reflection is stimulated by observations of the world around us, but a large proportion is also the result of self-interrogation and sifting through the trials and errors of which life is made. Whether we believe that life exhibits a definite unfolding pattern or is a large-scale drama in which we play a very small part or is merely a scene of irrational chaos in which we all must simply look after ourselves, people want to make sense of things in some kind of holistic fashion. As journalist Matthew Knott reflects, after having miraculously survived a five-storey fall from a New York building, "It seems to be part of human nature that when something momentous happens to us, we seek a deeper meaning in that event."[9] This effort involves both interior monologue and dialogue (or else actual conversation with others). Most of the time a clear cause and effect that govern events can be identified; yet few would deny that chance, luck, circumstance, or fate steps in from time to time. And it is then that we especially need to draw on our ability to put things into some significant perspective.

One of the major ways by which fate enters into our lives centres around relationships. In Sebastian Faulks' novel *Paris Echo*, the following exchange occurs between two of the main characters, with reference to a third who is now absent.

"'I don't know anyone in Paris …'

'What about your friend Sandrine?' said Hannah. 'Remember her?'

'I don't know how to find her,' I said. 'It's weird, she was part of my life, night and day, for a really important week or so and then … Nothing.'

'Life's like that, I'm afraid. Some chance meetings shape your whole existence. Others have no meaning at all.'"[10]

The factors that decide whether encounters have meaning and are formative in one's life are innumerable and therefore cannot be formulated with any precision. But what is evident is that such episodes are fateful, as are many of the circumstances and mini-incidents that make them either momentous or uneventful. So we have double-layered acts of fate here to consider, whereby meetings between people are both fortuitous and prove to be either forks in the road or non-starters. The role that unplanned encounters with others play in one's life can't be overemphasized. Humans are like randomly circulating particles, sometimes colliding, sometimes missing contact as we dash through the world and through time. But because we are deeply social beings and magnets of attraction and repulsion, chance meetings can be and often are of great importance and even lifelong resonance. Quite simply, they make us who we are, for good or bad, as much as any other influence.

It would be a fair generalization to say that life involves an ongoing monologue with oneself and many conversations with others about who we are and what we want, need, lack, and are willing or unwilling to work towards. These processes are notoriously variable from individual to individual and from moment to moment, and a lot of the momentum in one's life consists of reactions to developments and recalculations of where we're at in the pursuit of our goals. But, however we size up our point in time and future possibilities, there are some important constants in the mix too. As Oliver Burkeman observes, "The basic situation [for humans], the Buddha famously said, is that life is suffering. Everything is impermanent; old age, sickness and death are our inescapable fate. And your philosophy of happiness had better acknowledge these realities, otherwise the only possible result is even more suffering, for you and everyone around you."[11] This is why Buddhism encourages mindfulness (or being in the moment) – a focused awareness of what is going on around you *now*, how you are feeling and responding to it, and your capacity to change and adapt to it. We are neither chained to the past nor mere passive recipients of the unknown future. There is much that is beyond our control; but equally, we are often oblivious to the state we're in, our choices, and the potentials that reside within those choices.

The Fickle Finger of Fate

Both the capriciousness of fate's operation and our own capriciousness when interpreting its significance are noteworthy. People's remarks commonly tie their impression of fate's whimsy, in turn, to a perception of its relentless and mysterious blows and blessings. Simon Cleary's novel *The Comfort of Figs* centres on the construction of Brisbane's celebrated, heritage-listed Story Bridge, which opened in 1940. The lives of three workmen were lost while it was being built. During this period, one of Cleary's characters, a construction crew member, reflects, on behalf of his team, that "'it is not the dying that disturbs them, but that the engineers might already know the exact numbers. That the game is rigged. That the forces of fate can be documented in advance, history calculated according to some formula. It is this that feels like an abuse of trust. A blasphemy.'"[12] (This suspicion of "documentation in advance" seems to be confirmed by some papers an inquisitive workman steals from the field office.) Cleary later imagines a conversation between the bridge builder (O'Hara) and the bridge engineer (Lawrence) after completion of the project.

> "'Congratulations, Mr Lawrence …'
> 'It went off without a hitch in the end, didn't it?' O'Hara says.
> 'That it did.'
> 'According to plan?'
> 'Quite.'
> 'Did you expect any problems?'
> 'One never knows. One plans as well as one can, Mr O'Hara, and the rest is left in the hands of fate.'"[13]

This episode offers the tantalizing prospect that what appear to be fateful outcomes may sometimes be predictable. But even if it is common knowledge that bridge building is a dangerous job, we are left in suspense about the implacable factors in human endeavours for which allowance must be made. Nor is it clear how much allowance or what kind. This example suggests, too, a common perception that the negative impact of fate can be counted on to exact its toll, but no positive impact can be reasonably anticipated. As bridge engineer Lawrence contends, human planning – however much based on past experience and the best expertise available – can only take us so far, and the rest is impossible to control or foretell, residing in the realm of guesswork and hope. Such an approach to worldly affairs is very much in the spirit of the old saying, "man, indeed, proposes but God disposes, and God's way is not man's."[14]

Another, quite profound but also quirky and irreverent perspective on fate comes from a collection of short stories by Steven Millhauser. In one tale, the narrator observes,

> It sometimes happens that way: Fate blunders into a blind alley, and to everyone's embarrassment must pick itself up and try again. History too was always blundering … Yet perhaps they are not blunders at all, these false turnings, perhaps they are necessary developments in a pattern too complex to be grasped all at once. Or perhaps the truth was that there is no Fate, no pattern, nothing at all except a tired man looking back and

> forgetting everything but this and that detail which the very act of memory composes into a fate. Eschenburg [the story's protagonist], remembering his childhood, wondered whether Fate was merely a form of forgetfulness.[15]

There are several points of interest about this commentary. To begin with, it personifies fate as akin to humans, who have intentional intelligence but are also a bit clumsy and don't know their way about. People, according to this view, simply proceed by crude trial-and-error to seek the right path in life, or at least a reliable one. Next, history is likewise characterized. Then the author steps back and shifts to the now-familiar stance that fate really amounts to some kind of necessity lurking behind a masked reality, the impact of which is too intricate and subtle to comprehend. But just when this idea sinks in, a quite original notion is floated: that fate is merely an act of "forgetfulness," that is, a kind of trick played by selective memory, which betrays us into thinking that the events of life have some coherent meaning when actually they have none.

Taking a somewhat different tack, Bradford Morrow has a character in one of his novels observe that "Fate always operated, in my experience, with a most vivid sense of dark humor."[16] Israeli author Amos Oz also speaks of "a perverse fate that has willed" someone's misfortune.[17] Like other examples featured in the present chapter, these display the tendency, when thinking about fate, to personify it and even assign agency to it, as when we say a person willed such-and-such but "Fate had other ideas." The reasons for this are numerous, and a few have already been touched upon. Fate sometimes seems to be a crafty, working form of intelligence; other times it's more like a purveyor of jokes or ironies. It may pose a challenge we have to outwit, or an opportunity to be seized upon. In any event, fate is a factor that can either destabilize or stabilize the life course we are following.

Such thoughts return us, directly or indirectly, to a perception of ourselves as the playthings of a fated higher power – the evil or benign or simply unpredictable genius that intermittently dominates our lives. And at this juncture, we would do well to accept the advice of philosopher Arthur Schopenhauer. Despite his reputation as an arch-pessimist, Schopenhauer frequently offers pieces of wisdom that possess much value for the conduct of everyday life. He suggests that "Whatever fate befalls you, do not give way to great rejoicings or great lamentations; partly because all things are full of change, and your fortune may turn at any moment; partly because men are so apt to be deceived in their judgment as to what is good or bad for them."[18] Schopenhauer encourages us here to acknowledge not only that fate is precisely a phenomenon of change, but also, owing to its unpredictability, that it may swing from negative to positive impacts in an instant. He reminds us as well that we can see neither very far nor very accurately into the future, thus we cannot discern what sort of outcome events will eventually produce for us – or more importantly (we might add), what we will make of them. So we should take only a long, patient view of circumstances and events. This insight is potentially useful to everybody, from those facing the trials of everyday life to individuals contemplating suicide. In a similar vein, the ancient Roman lyric poet Horace (65–8 BCE) writes, "Drop the question what tomorrow may bring, and count as profit every day that Fate allows you."[19] These colourful remarks by great minds of the past underline a significant feature of talk about fate: that *when we invoke fate, we are very often trying to come to terms with the course of our lives as best we are able.*

Specialized Language

Having ventured this far into the land of fate, it should not surprise anyone that the notion upon which we have lavished so much attention has also been coopted, refined, and creatively reconfigured in order to perform relatively new conceptual tasks. Here's an illustration. Scientists and philosophers have studied and theorized about the maturation process of organisms for millennia. Over the past century and a half, biologists and embryologists have been tracing what is called the "fate map" of cells so as to gain a better grip on how they differentiate themselves over time. As researcher Corinne DeRuiter explains,

> Early development occurs in a highly organized and orchestrated manner … A chart or graphical representation detailing the fate of each part of an early embryo is referred to as a fate map. In essence, each fate map portrays the developmental history of each cell.
>
> Fate maps were developed as a way of tracing a particular region as it develops from an early embryo into a differentiated body plan. The first fate maps date back to the 1880s and in 1905 the first comprehensive collection of *Ascidian* (sea squirt) fate maps was published by Edwin Conklin. It is now common to find fate maps in introductory embryology texts …
>
> Creating a fate map is a valuable part of understanding an organism's developmental pathway … The possibility of new developmental discoveries comes with the creation of each new fate map.[20]

Historian Alice Wexler adopts the idea of a fate map as an image for framing her memoir/discussion (*Mapping Fate*) of what it is like to experience the weight of expectation and uncertainty surrounding a negative genetic inheritance.[21] Wexler, herself a 50/50 probability candidate for Huntington's disease (which is both incurable and fatal, and from which her mother died), details the cognitive and emotional dilemmas faced by those, like her, who wonder what the future holds for them. The Huntington's gene was discovered in 1993. Of those who have "undergone predictive testing" to discover their risk-level for contracting the disease, many experience a sense of foreboding and despair when receiving a positive result, which may be emotionally crippling. A smaller number redouble their efforts to make the most out of life, and some opt for no testing, preferring not to know their risk-level in the first place.[22] This shows, once again, that people's attitudes toward conditions of living that they cannot change are quite variable and far more complicated than the usual caricatures of fate would have us believe.

In Brief …

References to fate are an indelible part of everyday language and outlooks. Fate features in numerous figures of speech describing how life shapes up. These constructions can be found widely scattered throughout the realm of cultural products such as songs, novels, plays, and TV shows. While some people may invoke fate or fateful influences in order to evade responsibility for their own behaviours, fate's active operation or "unseen hand" is generally understood for what it is, namely, the incursion into our lives of unexpected, unavoidable events and factors that often radically change our personal direction or fortune.

4

FATEFUL ARGUMENTS

The ordinary use of language suggests that assertions about the future, just like assertions about the past, can be correct or incorrect. Therefore, this suggests that future-tense sentences, like past-tense sentences, can be true or false.

– Andrea Iacona[1]

Reason Weighs In

The perceived threat to human freedom is, for many, the chief worry generated by the idea of fate. This issue has spawned much of the fear of fate itself as well as the vast body of philosophical literature on fatalism. Before we get to this literature, however, recall once again that, as we saw in chapter 1, one can readily accept that there is such a thing as fate without embracing fatalism (which entails belief in fate's all-encompassing power). But hold on a minute. Perhaps the problem of undermining freedom doesn't vanish so swiftly. What if there really *is* a fixed order of things embedded in the nature of the universe, as fatalists argue? That would seem to be a game-changer. For if such a fixed order exists, then nothing you or anyone else can do will make any difference to the course of events. Some people have concluded from this that in any given situation, you might as well be passive and do nothing, or else do anything whatsoever that your momentary whim or impulse dictates – whether or not that behaviour is sensible or appropriate at the time. For example, if you're going to get hit by a car when crossing the street, and are *fated* to be hit whether you are careful or not, then it doesn't matter what approach you take. You can brazenly walk out in front of a speeding car or very judiciously pick a moment to cross; either way, it will make no difference to the outcome. You can also try to avoid crossing the street altogether in order to frustrate fate. But eventually you'll either judge it safe to cross (incorrectly, as it will turn out), or something – perhaps a child's cry for help – will intervene to make you forget your resolve and heedlessly cross the street. Again, the outcome will be what it will be. Any bold decision to cross over is not a matter of tempting fate, nor does any thoughtful self-restraint or act of taking care amount to thwarting fate, for fate already predetermines the result in question. In this manner a defeatist interpretation of events unfolds that is caricatured by both ancient and modern philosophers as "the lazy (or idle) argument." This is that in any set of circumstances, one might as well do nothing or act merely capriciously, since in the end it makes no difference to what happens, because *that* is out of one's control.

On an elementary, practical level, we all know that there is something wrong with this reasoning; what we do often *does* make a difference. We think it makes precisely *all* the difference – an assumption grounded in the cherished belief that our actions have consequences that flow ultimately from our own agency, intentions, and choices. For this reason, Stephen Hawking (1942–2018) sardonically remarks, "I have noticed even people who claim everything is predestined, and that we can do nothing to change it, look before they cross the road."[2] In a straightforward sense, then, we may suppose that fatalism – or at any rate a certain kind of adherence to fatalistic beliefs – is refuted by simple experience. But is it? What we witness above is only the response of those who think it doesn't matter, if fatalism is true, whether we engage actively with situations we find ourselves in, on the one hand, or lapse into a mode of passive, quiescent inaction or even thoughtless silliness, on the other. Surely, we think, no one would seriously endorse such a view, especially if she came to realize that it actually rests on an incorrect understanding of fatalistic belief. Philosopher Helena Eilstein points out that "A widespread misconception presents fatalism as a creed according to which certain events are going to happen *no matter what*, or, in other words, regardless of causes."[3] But it's precisely because most of us don't subscribe to an all-encompassing fatalism that we reject the lazy argument. We take it for granted that what people do (or omit to do) generally counts as part of the overall causal process by means of which events unfold.

And yet … the things we do and the choices we make sometimes trigger events or lead to circumstances that no one (especially we) could have predicted or controlled, and that may have far-reaching repercussions for ourselves and/or for others. Our lives sometimes veer in a direction that we have neither foreseen nor willed but which seems, retrospectively, as if it were inevitable. Because of this, though we may not be sold on fatalism, it's not that hard to identify, for instance, with the protagonist in Anthony Doerr's novel *About Grace*, who, at a certain stage of his life, despairs over "the possibility that it didn't matter what he had done, that outcome was independent of choice, that action or inaction, no decision mattered."[4] This sort of musing does not pretend to present an argument for fatalism, of course, but it may be the intuitive foundation upon which such arguments build. Everyone has pet theories, hunches, and suspicions about how the world works. And while fate may be closely allied with superstition and mythology within our own lives and in many traditions, there are also thinkers who have carefully constructed logical arguments leading to fateful conclusions. These arguments raise profound questions about how we think, about the nature of past, present, and future, and about truth claims concerning the world. In addition, certain ancient philosophers, although they have not left us with any well-rounded arguments, are nonetheless interpreted as having endorsed fatalistic views. These are reconstructed from surviving traces of their works, which generally comprise fragmentary sayings and second-hand reports of the positions they allegedly defended. Among this latter group are the pre-Socratics Heraclitus (c. 535–c. 475 BCE), Empedocles (c. 492–432 BCE), and Democritus (460–370 BCE).

Aristotle and the Sea Battle

Of greater significance than those views just mentioned, however, is the robust, well-honed case for fatalism. Mark Bernstein stresses that the more interesting and challenging kind of fatalism is a theory that has metaphysical or ontological implications, not merely logical or epistemic ones: "This fatalism is best seen as viewing the occurrence of all events, including future events, as necessary in just the same way as we commonsensically view the occurrence of past events. It views the future as being as closed as the past; just as we now have no ability to rearrange the furniture of the past, we likewise have no power to change the content of the future. Fatalistic necessity, then, is identified by the metaphysical fatalist with the necessity of the past, whereas the logical fatalist identifies it with the necessity of logic."[5] While it is true that fatalism is best understood as a metaphysical theory – a theory about what is the case, or about the nature of things – the most frequently formulated and debated arguments for fatalism nevertheless hinge on purely rational considerations. And many philosophers would argue that logical necessity carries over into determinations about the nature of reality.

Some arguments of this sort challenge reason itself to find a way out of what is perceived as a cul-de-sac where fatalism lurks. Others have it as their built-in aim to convince people that belief in fate – like fate itself – is unavoidable. Primary among the first group of thinkers, who've confronted fatalism head-on, is Aristotle (384–322 BCE), the most scientific and logically precise philosopher of ancient Greece and the major architect of fatalistic arguments in early Western thought. Aristotle ponders how we talk about future events.[6] He realizes that for any event, we may meaningfully state *now* that it either will or will not occur tomorrow. This is so independently of what eventually takes place tomorrow, because one of these two possibilities must be realized. That conclusion follows from a basic (bivalent) principle governing discourse called the "law of excluded middle": every statement is either true or false. In other words, it is universally and necessarily the case that for any statement we can make, if it is not true, then it is false, and vice-versa. Another way of saying the same thing is that for any proposition, either it is true or its negation is true. There aren't really any in-betweens or half-truths, according to this precept, only imprecise statements that can't properly be evaluated. Therefore, we are bound to observe the same rule if we want to communicate meaningfully with reference to the future, just as when we refer to the past and present.

Aristotle applies the law of excluded middle in the famous case of a hypothetical sea battle that seems to be an impending prospect somewhere for tomorrow. (He inherited this example from another ancient Greek thinker, Diodorus Cronus, who lived in the late fourth–early third centuries BCE.) Let's say that two individuals, Maria and Desirée, are arguing over this eventuality and making their respective claims about it. Maria posits that there will be a sea battle tomorrow and Desirée denies it. Aristotle suggests that their assertions are not merely predictions about what may or may not turn out to be true, as we might be accustomed to thinking. But what more could be at stake? Since they are statements concerning the world, philosophers would nowadays say that they possess "truth-value." This does not mean that they actually *are* true, just that they are (1) meaningful, (2) capable of being tested against the facts, and (3) such that in normal discourse, one of them must be true and the other false. An empirical statement's truth (or falsity) is a function of what it refers to or describes – that is, whether a certain state of affairs does or does not correspond to it. (For example, "The sky is blue" is true if and when the sky's color conforms to this statement, and false when it doesn't.)

But is the law of excluded middle a rule that governs statements concerning the future too? Could it be? Could it not be? If it necessarily applies, then either Maria or Desirée will prove correct in her belief about the sea battle, and we will have to wait until tomorrow to find out. So far, so good. However, the interesting question that surfaces at this point is the following: must it be either true or false *now* that there will be a sea battle tomorrow? Why would anyone think so? Initially this possibility strikes us as preposterous. After all, we customarily believe that the future is the realm of what is yet to happen, and that the future's coming-to-be is what makes all the difference. But *does* it make all the difference? Nobody seems to think that learning about the future is solely a matter of hanging around in order to see what will eventually take place. For one thing, we believe that human agency and natural events have a significant influence on how the future unfolds. Yet here, a deeper issue emerges.

We've seen that statements about the world must be either true or false. If so, then statements about the future can't be left floating in some kind of a truth-value limbo, because for statements to be *neither* true *nor* false is for them to be meaningless. So we seem to have two choices: Either statements about the future are meaningless, or else they have truth-value. Clearly they are not meaningless. But if they are meaningful (that is, have truth-value), then they must meet condition (3) above. Hence, every statement about the future, if it is meaningful, is either true or false *right now* (and was so in the past as well). It doesn't matter to the argument that we don't know at this point whether the sea battle will or won't occur. But it does begin to look as if the matter is out of our hands – or anyone else's – and will happen (or not) according to a pattern of determination that is somehow already set in the nature of things and that we are powerless to change. Indeed, according to Eilstein, it begins to look as if "for everything that ever occurs in the history of the universe there never was an instant when its occurrence was a mere possibility – a possibility that might fail to actualize."[7] Thus, the future appears to be in principle no different from past moments. We can't change the past, and each present moment instantly recedes into the fixed past, being replaced by a new and different present moment as time marches on. Is the future likewise beyond our grasp in terms of our ability to affect how it turns out?

An interesting sidelight of Aristotle's discussion is that the argument concerning the sea battle tomorrow may be thought to cast suspicion on the existence of free will in humans. But if so, it does this on purely logical grounds, not because of any conclusions regarding our basic nature, or any reflections on science, the laws of nature, mathematics, or anything related to these. Of course, any successful proof of an all-encompassing fatalism would crush belief in free will (and, among other things, moral responsibility). But the point here is that Aristotle's thoughts about fatalism remain standing independent of any controversy over the doctrine of determinism and its implications. (See discussion of fatalism and determinism in chapter 1.)

Some philosophers have attempted to dispense with the sea battle problem by means of what we might call a "common-sense" approach. Edward Craig, for instance, writes that it is essential "to address the crucial question about the direction of dependence: does the occurrence of the battle depend on the truth of today's statement, or the truth of today's statement on tomorrow's events?" He concludes in favour of the second option, which is "far more plausible."[8] Most of us would agree. But sometimes what we find obviously true or preferable breaks down under analysis to reveal a greater complexity or a hidden dilemma of thought or belief.

Aristotle's sea battle puzzle raises the subject of "future contingency," as it has come to be known. Most people would affirm that the future is an open realm of potentiality or possibility. Aristotle agrees, and hence concludes that statements about future events must be treated differently from those about past and present ones. For him, this leads to an escape route from fatalism. What happens currently or has happened is now fixed for all time, but what is yet to come might still turn out one way or another. Therefore, statements about what is yet to come must be regarded as unfixed with respect to their truth or falsity. They can, then, be true or false or not yet known to be either.[9] It remains the case that in the long run there either will or won't be a sea battle tomorrow (because one or the other of two contradictory statements must be true). However, there is no necessity in either direction, because logic governs statements, not events. Now if there's no necessity of events, then the sea battle argument poses no threat to personal freedom.[10] Aristotle thinks that this solution not only resolves the fatalism predicament but also makes references to the future more cogent, and renders us less prone to tying ourselves in logical knots when speaking in the future tense.

Discourse about the Future

Considerable controversy has surrounded the idea of future contingency, with other early Greek, Roman, and medieval scholars through the ages weighing in and either supporting or attacking Aristotle's proposed solution to the fatalism quandary. Part of the problem with Aristotle's approach is that it assumes a theory of truth that makes truth dependent on some corresponding fact(s) about the world. This may seem like a no-brainer. Yet it's easy to see that this cannot be the whole story about truth. For instance, we all accept that there are true statements about the past, of the type "Johnny was 175 centimeters tall when he went off in 1914 to fight in the First World War." But there is no present fact about the world, no current state of affairs, that makes this statement true when it is uttered here and now. Johnny no longer exists and this is why we are forced to say he *was* a specific height in 1914, or else to qualify our statement as corresponding to a past fact or a fact about the past. However, this move seems to entail that facts come and go on their merry way, as do the truths that depend upon them. But it surely strikes one as odd to conclude either that the statement just made about Johnny is no longer true, or else that it continues to be true even though its truth rests on a fact that no longer exists, or is merely a past fact that has faded away like the soldier himself. Similarly, we could say it is true that Jean Valjean (a character in Victor Hugo's novel *A Tale of Two Cities*) lived during the French Revolution. But since he's an imaginary person, what sort of truth does this statement have? Fictional truth, perhaps? You can see where this is going. If truth can't reliably rest on facts about the world, do we really want our ability to talk about the future to be contingent on currently nonexistent facts?

In the modern period, the Polish philosopher Jan Łukasiewicz (1878–1956) and others have defended the notion of "multivalued logics," or new ways of analyzing statements such as those about the future. Łukasiewicz himself was motivated partly by a wish to avoid fatalistic consequences such as we have been examining when he proposed a "three-valued logic," according to which statements are either true, false, or "indeterminate" (for example, possibly true or possibly false).[11] His system of logic has remained controversial, as have the commentaries and responses to Aristotle and other novel approaches over time, which demonstrates that the problem of fatalism refuses to go away and possesses an undeniably seductive allure. We also learn a deeper lesson from this example of the great power to disrupt our thinking and composure that resides within the notions of fate and fatalism. (Another disruption is the idea of an all-knowing God who apprehends past, present, and future simultaneously, which belief may also bring fatalism to the forefront, as we'll see in a moment.)

From Aristotle to Modern Times

Many important later thinkers grappled with the problem of fatalism, as noted earlier, including Seneca (c. 4 BCE–65 CE), Cicero, Boethius, St Augustine (354–430), Moses Maimonides (1135–1204), St Thomas Aquinas (1225–1274), William of Ockham (c. 1287–c. 1347), and Luis de Molina (1535–1600). The issues of interest, especially to the medieval philosophers on this list, revolve around the concept of divine foreknowledge (or omniscience), which seems to block the possibility of human free will. Why so? Because if God knows in advance whatever is or will ever be true (or false) about the world, then any actions not in conformity with what God knows would threaten to undermine the claim of divine omniscience, denying God's very nature or essence. Philosophical theologians have worried about this matter because they wanted both to posit an omniscient deity who controls everything, and also to depict humans as beings with free will, who can decide their own destiny and choose to follow either the path of righteousness or that of sinfulness. (We will return to the omniscience problem shortly.)

A Different Avenue to Fatalism

The second type of argument – referred to earlier as "perverse" – is committed to proving that fatalism is *actually true*, or at any rate that it is an inescapable inference from basic presuppositions of everyday reasoning. This approach revisits the problem Aristotle wrestled with, but in a more systematic way that ends by concluding that we're trapped, by beliefs we cannot avoid relying on, into accepting fatalism. It follows that our behaviours are unavoidable, and that we cannot in all honesty think otherwise. So what we consider to be our range of choices consists of merely various fictitious, apparent, spurious alternatives and, like events that have already taken place, are things no one has the power to change.

A contemporary philosopher who argues in this way is Richard Taylor, whom we met briefly in chapter 1. Taylor launched two major attempts to clinch the case for fatalism. In his earlier (and very controversial) approach to the problem, Taylor begins with the point – obvious to everyone – that each statement about the past is either true or false. Statements about the past are never "indeterminate," unless we mean by this that either memory or historical knowledge falls short of capturing their essence. If a statement about the past is true, no one can alter its truth; if false, its falsity is likewise fixed forever. "A fatalist," Taylor now tells us, "thinks of the future in the manner in which we all think of the past,"[12] namely, as immutable. Taylor next presses upon us the assumption (which he holds we all make) "that time is not by itself 'efficacious'; that is, that the mere passage of time does not augment or diminish the capacities of anything and, in particular, that it does not enhance or decrease an agent's powers or abilities." Any changes in an agent's powers or abilities – or in anything else for that matter – "is always the result of something other than the mere passage of time."[13] Furthermore, whatever anyone has the power or ability to do (or not to do) – call it X – depends in general on the existence of a certain range of conditions necessary for doing (or not doing) X. But if, in referring to X, we are talking about something in the future – for example that I will go to the movies tomorrow – then it is either true or false that I will go to the movies tomorrow. If the conditions (now) exist for me to go to the movies tomorrow, then it is true that I will go, and no power or ability of mine can or will change that outcome. Likewise, if the conditions do not exist, no power or ability of mine can or will enable me to go. If time (or the passage of time) alone changes nothing, then does it perhaps follow that statements about the future are true or false, in a tenseless sense – that is, true or false always and forever?

Taylor's later argument for fatalism runs roughly as follows. Every statement is either true or false. What is true doesn't "become" true with the passage of time; rather, whatever will eventually be seen to be true is merely what has always been true, although we didn't know it (yet). Therefore, every future state of things is unavoidable, and only human belief in freedom and ignorance makes us think things could happen otherwise than they do.[14]

An Instructive Tale

Taylor offers a cautionary fictitious story concerning a man named Osmo, who discovers a musty old library book which, to Osmo's astonishment and dismay, records his biography exactly as it has unfolded – and, more significantly, the full details of his future life. Perusing this volume, Osmo reads about his impending tragic demise in a plane crash some three years hence, and we learn that, as it happens and in spite of his frantic efforts to avoid this outcome, his own last-minute actions actually cause the final event to occur. Taylor's point is that, just as poor Osmo's life had been summarized by some unknown author in a book hitherto unknown to him, so too there exists a "book" of such "truths" for each of us, making our lives fated in just the same general manner. That's because there is a set of true statements (some about the past, others about the present, and still others about the future) that summarizes the course of every person's life (just as, of course, there is a set of false statements that does not). Such a set exists for the reason that every statement describing any moment of one's life is either true or false, and the sum total of the true statements constitutes what might be called the timeless story of one's life. (From the standpoint of an all-knowing mind, it could be added, this set of statements could be laid out as if sketched on a flat surface where they can all be seen instantaneously as both true and, as it were, *simultaneously present.*) The most important insight to retain in all of this is that whether we know of such a book or not, or have ever encountered it, is irrelevant to the argument for fatalism. The only thing that matters is that for each of us there does exist a complete set of true statements describing the course of her or his life.[15]

A Model of Fatalism: The Self-Fulfilling Prophecy

The story of Osmo is but another instance of a particular literary and mythological trope that revolves about the theme of fatalism. In ancient Greek tragedy, many heroes faced consequences for their actions. Oedipus, mythical king of Thebes, for example, was prophesied to kill his father Laius and marry his mother Jocasta in the drama by Sophocles (c. 496–406 BCE). Notwithstanding that he strives to ensure that this does *not* come to pass, Oedipus falls into the snare of events that fate has set for him and ends up fulfilling the prophecy.[16] Similarly, in a modern play by British author W. Somerset Maugham (1874–1965), there is a retelling of the "appointment in Samarra" fable – an ancient story of fatal entrapment that first appears in the Jewish text known as the Babylonian Talmud (fourth century CE). The story goes as follows: a merchant's servant is confronted in a Baghdad marketplace by the personified figure of Death. In a panic, he borrows the merchant's horse in order to flee to Samarra and thereby avoid Death. Later the same day, the servant's master also encounters Death, who remarks of the man's servant, "I was astonished to see him in Baghdad, for I had an appointment with him tonight in Samarra."[17] Characteristic of all such tales is that their protagonists are powerless to prevent a certain outcome from occurring; but in some of them, there is the additional wrinkle that (like Osmo) they also unwittingly bring about what it is they vainly struggle to avoid. The notion that individuals' personal fates are inscribed in a book somewhere is also echoed in Islamic tradition: Abd-al-Hosayn Zarrinkub cites both the Qur'an and Hadith to illustrate a belief that "whatever happens in the world has been written down by God with the Pen of the Divine Will on the Tablet of the Eternal Decree" and is therefore "immutable."[18]

Divine Omniscience and Omnipotence

Monotheistic religions – Judaism, Christianity, and Islam – feature an all-knowing, all-powerful deity. In Christianity, for example, disciples of Christ note that "God's will be done."[19] Other references reinforce this stricture: "For I have come down from heaven, not to do my own will but the will of him who sent me."[20]

There are both believers and non-believers in these faiths who have argued that this conception of God leads to fatalism. Let's see why. An omniscient God, who is the creator of all that exists, will be able to apprehend past, present, and future in the same instant (as noted earlier in this chapter), and to know in advance everything that is going to happen. Such a God created the world as it was, is, and will be, and so, as events unfold, there are no surprises from the deity's point of view. Now if we shift the focus to human actions, we find that each of these is part of God's preordained plan – whatever it might be – and cannot deviate from it. God foresees all deeds and their outcomes and has the power to alter or eternally preserve anything along the way. It matters not whether God chooses at certain points to revise his/her plan because such an intervention would likewise override human choice in the same manner, namely, by changing the plot that we act out according to divine specifications.[21]

Theistic defenders of human freedom urge that while God foresees what people will do, the divine nature does not predetermine it. Having given humans free will, the theists argue, God has also granted them the capacity to make independent choices (as in the Garden of Eden). Being omniscient, and apprehending all events timelessly, God can predict what choices will be made, and is therefore a sorrowful witness to our fallibility. As a defense against fatalism, however, this clearly won't do. Why not? Because God is not only the all-seeing *observer* of what happens, but also the *creator* of exactly such beings that (as God can eternally foretell) will make just such choices. The appearance of freedom is supported by God's decision not to intervene in order to prevent tragedies from taking place (for example), or more generally, not to circumscribe in any way the course individual human lives are to follow. But perhaps God does sometimes intervene to save a nation or an individual that is in acute distress (such as the ancient tribes of Israel, as in the Bible). Unfortunately, this does not improve the overall picture, for the reason that we now have the following situation: God (being omniscient) knew in advance that he/she would intervene at this moment; and God's intervention charts a new (known-in-advance) course for people to act out.[22] Both of these conditions, however, seem to yield new fatalistic scenarios of an inescapable sort.

In Brief …

It seems, then, that when confronted by the problem of fatalistic belief, reason is bound to tie itself into knots. This is a sobering realization because it indicates that fatalism can be neither definitively proved nor refuted. Fatalism will continue to hover in the background, for most of us, like a bad smell or an unwanted guest. Consequently, any meaningful perspective on fatalism will have to be based on life experience and reflective examination of it. Those who have argued for fatalism claim that it is inescapable and try to show this by means of deductive argumentation. But this whole approach fails to do justice to the way in which real life events may be seen as ineluctable. That has to do with the fact that when a path is chosen or a momentous opportunity or adversity appears out of the blue, the direction one's life takes in response opens up. But following one course also closes other directions that might have been taken or revealed, in a kind of chain of indiscernible connections and disconnections. A convenient image to think of here is that of a tree chart that shows how various alternatives lead to different or opposite subalternatives, and these to different or opposite sub-sub-alternatives, possibly ad infinitum. However, since life is rather too fluid to be captured by such a static representation, perhaps imagining ripples on a pond when a stone is cast into the water is a better way to visualize fate's far-reaching effects. From this reflection on what seems to be the inevitability of fate, we may even derive a "proof" that fate to some extent governs people's lives. Not the kind of proof that philosophers defending fatalism covet, to be sure – for that concludes with our inability ever to be able to change anything or take responsibility for our lives. No, what we have here instead is the affirmation that since we are all born into a fateful condition (signified by our place in time, genetic heritage, sex, and so on), and personally experience unforeseen, often momentously impacting events, then our lives contain a central element of fate that has many and widening repercussions. It doesn't follow, however, that we can't take charge of this process in a meaningful fashion, as chapter 6 explains.

5

A TOOL FOR SOCIAL CONTROL

All who are not of good race in this world are chaff.
– Adolf Hitler[1]

Fate, or Providence, will give the victory to those who most deserve it.
– Adolf Hitler[2]

Fate as Ideology

Jean-Paul Sartre (1905–1980), arch-defender of personal and political freedom, observes that "There are indeed many precautions to imprison a man in what he is, as if we lived in perpetual fear that he might escape from it, that he might break away and suddenly elude his condition."[3] Sartre argues passionately that it is our responsibility to fight against these "imprisonments" and promote a life of agency, self-assertion, and dignity for ourselves and others.

We all have fixed parameters in our lives – firstly, those given elements we start out with (chiefly our genetic inheritance, our time and place of birth, and the inevitability of growing older); and secondly, those we acquire (such as diseases or injuries). Even someone so immersed in defending freedom of choice and creative self-development as Sartre admits that who we are is partly defined by these unchangeable elements. But no one's essence need be set in stone by either inherited or acquired factors. In the end, it's what we do with our endowments and limitations that defines our lives. There are many caring people – like good parents, teachers, friends, and partners – who encourage and support others' self-making activities and their attempts to triumph over adversity. However, there are also unfortunately many who focus on doing the opposite. Innate characteristics as well as circumstances beyond people's choice or control have been used as grounds for suppressing or eliminating their freedom and have even cost them their lives. Fate may be featured in the foreground or hover in the background of belief systems and discussions about human nature, but it is likewise often drawn into efforts aimed at making people feel and act in subservient ways. This is the downside of fate's history. We will look at a few important examples of this lamentable record in order to gain a more complete picture of fate's ability to influence thought and action. This will also give us better ideas and intuitions about how we can transcend fate.

Biology and Destiny

Sex

Sexuality (maleness or femaleness) is evidently a bedrock condition of humanity, as are gayness, intersexuality, and transgenderedness. These aspects of identity seem to be fated just as much as birth and death. Sexual bigotry, which usually assumes male heterosexuality as the norm and ideal, is still widespread across the globe. Its effects – principally the devaluing, abuse, inequality, and second-class standing of women – stand out as persistent social problems. That girls and women in many countries experience unequal treatment – in the workplace, in wage structures, before the law, in social and family situations, in religious narratives and practices, in political representation, in educational opportunities, and in many other areas – is both well known and empirically established. And yet these forms of injustice remain. Violence against girls and women is historically unremitting in both peacetime and wartime. Although there has been progress toward improving the prospects of females in different parts of the world, many still lack the autonomy to decide their own future. The overall situation is dire, not only because it degradingly affects half of humanity, but also because educating and empowering women is a significant investment in promoting peace, security, democracy, and prosperity.[4] Men, too, benefit significantly from sexual equality.[5]

Sexism or misogyny calls for explanation as a type of phobia that leads to prejudice, discrimination, intimidation, gratuitous violence, and restricted personal development and opportunities. An adequate account of these dynamics is bound to be complex, because it involves reference to institutionalized social attitudes, gender roles and expectations, political power struggles, and a host of other factors. But any thoroughgoing analysis also needs to acknowledge that sexism primarily feeds on the unconscious, unspoken assumption that some people are less deserving because of the biological category to which they belong.

Other forms of sexual discrimination (both social and legal) rife in the world today are equally subject to this analysis. These have more to do with genetically predisposed gender identifications than just biological maleness and femaleness. According to one research source, seventy-one countries currently have anti-gay laws,[6] and at the time of writing, one of these (Uganda) has just passed a law creating new offenses that are punishable by life imprisonment and even the death penalty.[7]

Race

Race membership, as a way of identifying, emphasizing, and evaluating human differences, is at least as old as recorded history. Racial typology was solemnly codified in encyclopedias and other reference works and taught in schools as factual until very recently. The concept of race used to be taken as a self-evident category even by many respectable thinkers. But it is now known to be scientifically unfounded and merely a shabby social construct, a bad habit of biased observation that is often driven by unconscious bigotry as well as hidden agendas of domination and exploitation.

Racism is a multilayered ideology, which is parasitic on foundational assumptions about people, and it generally comprises a judgmental and discriminatory outlook, accompanied by emotive attitudes such as dislike or hatred and various forms of vilification, exploitation, and ostracism based on the supposed inferiority of the target group. According to racists, "members of their own race are mentally, physically, morally, or culturally superior to those of other races."[8] Historian Russell McGregor observes that in the late nineteenth and early twentieth centuries, it became a "scientific axiom" that certain races, presumed by learned investigators to be primitive and therefore inferior from an evolutionary point of view (such as Australian Aborigines or African Pygmies), are doomed (or fated) to die out.[9] To many, this seemed to follow logically from the concept of the "survival of the fittest," posited by Charles Darwin (1809–1882).

Such malignant ideas have been embedded in social and political discourse, and have motivated behaviours ranging from stereotyping to segregation, and from colonial exploitation to enslavement, murder, and genocide. It almost goes without saying that these practices can be and often are systemic or institutionalized, meaning that they become part of "the way things are done" – the explicit or implicit rules and policies by which a society operates, advantaging some over others. During the period of slavery in the United States, for example, laws were passed that enforced the property status of slaves, and even afterwards some laws continued to block "interracial" marriage for decades. Literacy was denied to slaves as well. The South African apartheid system meticulously defined gradations of racial membership and regulated the rights and privileges of those so classified. And in Nazi Germany, racist mythology, caricatures, and data from personal and ancestral records were used to create and sustain an elaborate system of legal and extralegal abuse that poisoned every aspect of daily life.

Racism's ugly history is still unfolding, notwithstanding the fact that its basic premises have been repeatedly shown to be epistemologically empty and morally bankrupt. In addition, as has recently been exposed, racism sadly continues to infect social research to an alarming degree.[10] (See "Fraudulent Genetics," below.) That it hovers just beneath the threshold of everyday consciousness was dramatically illustrated in 2020 by worldwide demonstrations and riots sparked off by police killings of Black citizens in the US and elsewhere.

Racist behaviour is not only empirically unfounded but also morally wrong because it contravenes numerous standards that are essential to any well-considered ethical viewpoint, such as fairness, kindness, empathy, and compassion, as well as the general notion of equality. It may be added that racism leads to discrimination on the basis of characteristics that (some) people possess for reasons beyond their control – that are part of their individual fates, for which they can hardly be blamed.

Caste

Within the human community, socioeconomic class distinctions are some of the most universal and persistent divisions used to define a person's identity. These have to do mostly with ritual status, wealth, power, and honour. Mobility among classes or, by contrast, rigidity of membership criteria, varies among groups and at different places and times. Class identity may be marked by fluidity, as we acknowledge when using expressions like "social climber," "upwardly mobile," or "nouveau riche" to describe certain individuals and their lifestyles. Whether this change of status is more apparent than real in societies that at least notionally value equality among their members may be debated. So may the question whether some economic disparities have evolved in more of a de facto manner than as a result of deliberate arrangements dictated by power and privilege. But what cannot be challenged is that many groups throughout history have enforced upon their members the most inflexible class systems imaginable.

An example from today's world is provided by the group known in India as "untouchables" (or *dalit*). According to one source, "At the beginning of the twenty-first century there are well over 160 million untouchables on the Indian subcontinent ... their low position deriving from the belief that they embody extreme impurity ... Strong links between their religious and social subordination and their widespread poverty and economic exploitation make untouchables some of the most disadvantaged groups in South Asia."[11] Although untouchability became an illegal designation after the 1948 Indian liberation from colonial rule and the birth of independence, traditional discrimination and self-defining practices nevertheless continue. While most untouchables are Hindus, those who have converted to other religions remain tainted by their original biological inheritance. This underlines the permanency of caste membership, which is a very complicated phenomenon. Many social, political, historical, religious, regional, and other factors are at work both externally and internally to the untouchable community, defining what it means to belong to it, changing the meaning of this identity over time, and creating systems of sub-castes. Ideas about residual bad karma resulting from conduct in one's previous lives also help to maintain caste membership (whether high or low) as a kind of "deserved outcome."

In practical terms, untouchables are targeted by fixed codes of conduct that restrict types of clothing, modes of transport, access to religious sites and priests, dwelling locations, and symbolic interactions with other members of the larger society. In like manner, untouchables have been relegated to the most horrendous forms of employment, such as dealing with dead animals and accumulations of human waste of all types, scavenging, leather manufacture, work at cremation sites, and other kinds of contact with highly polluting and unhygienic materials, as well as performing landless agricultural labour. Of course, these activities reinforce the labelling of untouchables, since – however essential it may be – the work involved is avoided by everyone else and held in the lowest regard. Consequently, people of other castes shun those who perform these tasks. *Dalit* women also suffer sexual and economic exploitation by men of "higher" caste membership.

There has been a lengthy struggle by untouchables to claim human rights, fair treatment, and greater political power, as well as to define themselves in their own terms. These tendencies are in conflict with other ones, because "within the untouchable religions [as they have developed,] the unequal relationships and ritual power at the core of caste have been reproduced and reconfigured."[12] In other words, the stereotyped identity projected from the outside onto a group such as this becomes internalized by group members themselves, and it is also ingrained via repetitive performance of those daily activities described above. Thus, a way of life becomes transformed into a perpetually solidified self-image. And unfortunately, in this setting as elsewhere, low self-esteem and depression act as triggers for self-fulfilling prophecies, so that, among other things, people often act out stereotypes they have been conditioned to believe in.

In ancient slave-based societies, many of which had hereditary, divinely approved rulers, the opportunity for social mobility and improvement in status across generations was often minimal or non-existent (as observed in chapter 2). But even in more recent times, numerous caste-like social arrangements have been identified, featuring rigid class systems with inherited and built-in modes of underprivilege. Just to take one example, during the shogun-and-samurai Tokugawa period of Japan's history (1603–1867), there existed a social hierarchy with an outcast group at the bottom who faced restrictions similar to those experienced by India's untouchables.[13] Historical illustrations can be plentifully multiplied, of course. English bigotry directed against the Irish ranged from cruel representations, to religious discrimination, to denial of employment opportunities and failure to relieve the tragic potato famine during the Victorian period. And Black Africans in America suffered the cruel deprivations of slavery, while an entire economy and beneficial way of life for white people was built on the backs of Black labour.

Fate is the lens that brings this picture into focus both for those making the judgment that pronounces on who is an outcast, and for those experiencing the pronouncement's burdensome effects. Negative impacts on the present generation also transfer to their offspring, who acquire the condition of their parents without any say in the matter. ("Once an outcast, always an outcast." "Like father, like son." "The apple doesn't fall far from the tree." "What can be expected from people of that type?") The hand of fate delivers exclusion, oppression, and exploitation to those whose only crime was being born and/or having inherited certain visible traits. But of course, it likewise delivers good fortune, with equal largesse, to those who are born well; and to the majority who find themselves in the middle, it brings safety from the extremes.

Fraudulent Genetics

We live in a time when scientific understanding of the genetic basis of life-forms (including our own) is advancing exponentially, and astonishing new discoveries are rapidly accumulating. According to the Human Genome Project, for example, humans are now known to be 99.9 per cent genetically identical to one another.[14] What about the other one-tenth of a per cent? How much of an impact does it have? Behavioural geneticist Robert Plomin argues that "inherited DNA differences are the main reason why we are who we are."[15] These differences are "systematic, stable and long-lasting,"[16] in contrast to the random factors of life that each of us encounters along the way, our individual conditioning, and even, apparently, the social construction of experience and our general outlook on reality. Plomin reckons it has already been proved that 50 per cent of our psychological makeup is determined by heredity – far more than by any non-hereditary item or condition. The other ingredient usually cited in these discussions – "environment" or "nurture" – includes diverse elements, to be sure; but he alleges that many of the non-hereditary factors making us who we are come about because traits that we've acquired by heredity also heavily influence the life choices we make. He urges, finally, that more detailed ("polygenic") analysis of individuals' DNA profiles "can predict adult traits from infancy."[17]

In spite of all this, Plomin nevertheless denies that genetics is destiny and urges that no social policy implications follow from these findings. Social policy is, rather, the product of values we bring to the table. Assuming that the conclusions he reports were well-established (though they are still subject to much debate), what *does* follow? This is a very big question, which we cannot resolve here; but the trouble is that such large-scale, provocative discoveries lend themselves to abuse as readily as to constructive ends. And politicians plus others with their own agendas have been only too eager to exploit various avenues to social control.

One important form of intellectual and social tendency in which fate hovers in the not-so-distant background is the eugenics movement. Beginning with the writings of Francis Galton (1822–1911), it soon spread from his native England around the world, and was particularly influential in the United States and Germany during the early to mid-twentieth century. Eugenics advocates observed that while humans lavished excessive attention on the proper breeding of livestock and plants, they neglected the obvious opportunity to improve their own species through selective breeding. Eugenicists argued that such selective breeding was a viable option for creating a better future.

If ever there has existed a full-blown application of the idea that "biology is destiny," eugenics would have to be it. Eugenics promoters did not baldly teach that heredity is everything, but they did hold that it is the primary determining and unchangeable factor for many social and behavioural problems, the causes of which may be traced to reproduction by "defective and degenerate people." This broad-brush characterization is owing to the very mixed set of issues the eugenicists focused on, including "insanity, feeblemindedness, epilepsy, pauperism, alcoholism and certain forms of criminality."[18] The concept of "better human breeding" led to the establishment of a number of research centres and data collection resources in England, the US, and Europe, and prominent eugenics proponents were members of the professorial and administrative staff at numerous front-rank universities during the first half of the twentieth century.

Eugenics research was conducted with enthusiasm for many decades. But from fairly early on critics began to spotlight poor experimental design, methodological flaws, sloppy data collection, inaccuracy, overgeneralization, and cultural bias – the hallmarks of unscientific claptrap. Many problems – probably or likely caused by social disadvantage and environment, or by a complex combination of factors – were simplistically attributed to heredity instead. Nevertheless, the influence of eugenics research continued well into the 1920s and 30s, with the US Congress passing legislation designed to weed out would-be immigrants springing from "defective gene pools," and several states adopting sterilization laws. Inmates of mental and penal institutions were the prime targets of those state laws, and over sixty thousand persons were sterilized by the 1960s. (A similar number were sterilized in Sweden during roughly the same period.) Forced sterilization laws were enacted in most US states and persisted into the present century.[19] In Germany, four hundred thousand people were involuntarily neutered during the 1930s. What is perhaps not so widely known is that US legislation was used as the foundation for Nazi-era German law, and that Adolf Hitler (1889–1945) both embraced America's racist history and admired the American eugenics movement.[20]

The Second World War became the apex period for racial discrimination via eugenics, with the Nazi regime designating as "unfit" or "undesirable" various human groups, based on real or imagined characteristics shared by their members. "Negative eugenics," such as involuntary euthanasia and sterilization or marriage restriction, was also accompanied by the "positive eugenics" of encouraging breeding among "superior" races' finest representatives. Eugenics run amok paved the way for the systematic genocide of the Holocaust. While Jewish people were the primary target of the extermination camps (most estimates state that approximately six million Jews lost their lives), many other groups were systematically murdered as well. The list of additional victims comprises Roma, Sinti, people with mental or physical disabilities, "subhuman" Slavs (such as Poles and captured Russian soldiers), Jehovah's Witnesses, suspected homosexuals, and assorted "asocials" (homeless people, those on welfare, sex workers, beggars, alcoholics, and drug addicts).[21] As can readily be discerned, most of these groups of individuals were persecuted owing to their fated identities.

Nazi genocide was very extreme, but there have been and still are many other examples across the globe. Going beyond this phenomenon, it needs to be noted here more generally that war, which usually takes place between conflicting ethnic groups, is fought by combatants conditioned to kill fellow human beings they have been led to stereotype as "enemies," who have usually done no wrong to them personally, and whose only "crime" is having been assigned a contrasting identity by the hand of fate. Propaganda is well known and well-studied as the vehicle for promoting negative images and mindless hatred of those who are different as well as for glorifying war and creating mythologies of racial/cultural superiority.

Finally, DNA samples are being used by the Chinese government to identify members of Han, Tibetan, Uighur Muslim, and other ethnic groups believed to contain dissidents, activists, and terrorists, in what is considered to be a widespread "campaign of surveillance and oppression."[22] A network of detention and brainwashing centres is revealed in the secret "China Cables," published in 2019.[23] Meanwhile more recent reports document forced sterilization, abortion, torture, and sexual abuse imposed on Uighur women.[24] Tests to distinguish between people belonging to one ethnic group or another have been developed, using technology purchased from US firms and acquired from American researchers, as well as data from an openly accessible global collection of genetic information (the 1000 Genomes Project). This is all part of a larger plan – already manifested in the persecution, intimidation, and incarceration of people in "re-education" camps – to transform these groups into loyal government supporters.[25] The objective of the DNA collection effort seems to be to build a massive database that will aid in creating a docile, more uniform population. In addition to the violation of human rights through the forcible and clandestine collection of genetic material, this process also contravenes scientific/ethical norms requiring informed consent from those who yield personal information of various types.

The lesson learned from this example is that if your fate is being a genetically identifiable Uighur, Tibetan, or Han individual living in China, you may expect to be systematically discriminated against. Likewise, those who are fated to be born and identified as Rohingya (in Myanmar), Roma (just about anywhere), ethnic Armenians in the Ottoman Empire (1914–23), or Tutsi (during 1994 in the Rwandan Civil War) face, or have faced, anything from persecution to genocide, even without being singled out by genetic testing. The same applies to many other ethnic groups too numerous to list here.

Now, just for the record, what if eugenics were "good science" rather than being fraudulent? This might mean, for example, that racial, gender, or ethnic membership could be empirically linked with traits such as likelihood of certain types of criminal or antisocial behaviour. In a just society, it would remain subject to debate whether the principles of rightness and fairness permitted this information about people's fated inheritance to be ferreted out and socially applied at all. And if it were to be used, debate would have to centre on equally important subsidiary questions, such as which ends it should serve, and who should have the authority to decide on these issues and to implement decisions regarding them. For the basic moral idea operative here is that people ought not to be held responsible, punished in advance, or otherwise ostracized for possessing properties that they cannot help having. A just and decent society respects this principle and promotes as well the capacity of each to freely shape a life against the background of whatever conditions have been given to that individual.

Predestination

The idea of predestination leads us into another complex arena of fate-driven social control. Predestination is the notion that God has decided, in advance of humans' lives being led, who will be selected to receive salvation in the afterlife. While this view is often identified with a particular strand of Protestant Christianity (Calvinism, as explained below), it has much earlier roots in the biblical utterances of St Paul (died c. 62–64 CE) and the theological writings of St Augustine, St Thomas Aquinas, and others. Some locate the origins of predestination even further back, in the Old Testament story of the nation of Israel as the promised and destined location of God's "chosen people."[26] Christian thinkers have wrangled throughout the ages over the grounds for making claims about predestination, and some of the best minds have engaged in extreme forms of mental gymnastics over this topic.[27] Predestination is often said to result from God's foreknowledge of human choices, with salvation being awarded to those whom God knew would lead a righteous life. But according to certain viewpoints, God's mercy and grace are also factors, although the bestowal of these gifts could be predestined as well. Some believe that damnation, to which the failure of salvation leads, can be avoided by steadfast faith and/or good deeds that elicit God's compassion and grace. But others deny this, holding that divine largesse is "gratuitous," which leads to the notion of God's showing active favouritism.[28] And finally, there are those who argue that humans as a whole are "doubly predestined" because God selects one part of our species for salvation and another for damnation. Much convoluted reasoning has been applied to the question of reconciling human free will and divine predestination.[29]

In Christianity, the idea that salvation comes to the faithful via God's grace (which might be thought of as a fateful dispensation) is strongly associated with Martin Luther (1483–1546) and John Calvin (1509–1564). In historical accounts predestination is linked more particularly with Calvin, although some caution is necessary, for as Brian Armstrong argues, it is "presented by Calvin as the response or affirmation of a man of faith, affirming the control of God in his life, not as an epistemological program."[30] This underlines the fact that Calvin's theology is more practical than theoretical in character and intent. Modern scholarship therefore inclines toward the view that predestination represents an important preoccupation of Calvinism, rather than its central precept. Nevertheless, there is no denying the formative influence of this doctrine within Calvinist Protestantism. As Calvin himself states, "We call predestination God's eternal decree, by which he determined with himself what he willed to become of each man. For all are not created in equal condition; rather, eternal life is foreordained for some, eternal damnation for others."[31] Humans are sinful, fallen beings who have fatefully inherited original sin. Such beings can only hope to achieve redemption through religious subservience; it is God alone, then, who ordains the ultimate outcome of a person's striving, and God does so even prior to creating the universe.

Aside from the significant degree of social control exerted within a community of worshippers by any strict and uncompromising system of religious beliefs and practices, Calvinism has had a major impact on several European countries, the UK, and the US. This creed took root in Geneva to the extent of becoming the foundation of both political and religious life. During the sixteenth century, in the name of Calvinist principles, people were tried for blasphemy, banished, beheaded, and burnt at the stake (most odiously, the Spanish Renaissance humanist Michael Servetus, who lived 1511–1553). The Synod of Dort (Dordrecht), held by the Dutch Reformed Church in 1618–19, reaffirmed predestination against the Arminian theological movement, stimulating continued repression of the latter by the former.

Not long after, the Westminster Confession of Faith was convened in response to a call from the Parliament of England. Its brief was to standardize Christian dogma for the Church of England. This council's deliverances in 1647 widely influenced other Protestant denominations and included a reaffirmation of double predestination.

With these events occurring all around them, ordinary citizens in many countries would have cowered before the authoritarian elites of their time. For individuals' inherent uncertainty whether they were among those selected to attain salvation rather than damnation exerted a very high pressure on them to adhere to their religion's teachings and to conform to the way of life it prescribes, as defined and codified by its leaders, who thus became enforcers.

Beliefs about predestination also exist in the Arab world, and are known to predate Islam. These concern the day of one's death and one's allotment of food.[32] Numerous passages in the Qur'an suggest that Allah selects outcomes in advance, or at any rate independent of human choice – most notably, each person's time of death.[33] A central example is found in this frequently uttered prescriptive admonition: "And never say of anything, 'I will definitely do this tomorrow,' without adding, 'if Allah so wills! (*inshallah*).'"[34] Julian Baggini, in his worldwide overview of comparative philosophy, explains the meaning of the relevant scriptural statements as follows: "God's control is such that nothing happens unless he wills it, which results in a strong strand of belief in predestination."[35] This interpretation is confirmed by Islamic scholar Helmer Ringgren, who writes that according to several traditions of Islam, "God's decree is infallibly fulfilled and no human effort can ward it off or change it."[36] This leaves room for naturalistic explanations of many behaviours and events, although ultimately fate rules.

These fatalistic mindsets suggest that in certain cultural settings fate is thought to prevail at all times, or at least more often than not. We might call the state of things that such beliefs refer to as "the inevitability of inevitability": everything hangs in the balance and one can never be truly sure of an outcome's likelihood until it actually happens. Furthermore, it is always possible that some cosmic influence outside of oneself is the real efficacious agency.

But theorists have not been at a loss to explain how humans can remain free and responsible even within *this* apparently restrictive philosophical framework. Both Christian and Islamic traditions feature considerable bodies of commentary explaining how bad behaviour is eventually traceable to human choice alone, with divine retribution often being the consequence. Thus, for example, the early Islamic theologian al-Hasan al-Basri (642–728) is said to argue "that the fact that God knows that some people will disbelieve is only descriptive; that is, he knows that by their own free choice they will disbelieve, but his knowledge does not predetermine their unbelief ... In this way, [al-Hasan al-Basri] can maintain that God creates only good and that evil comes from human beings or from Satan."[37] The explanatory strategy here is to assume that Allah controls not specific human choices and acts but only their outcomes. Occasionally the deity promotes good self-making through salvific acts of grace. But a monotheistic god who really isn't in time anyway (being eternal and having pre-existed and created time) cannot be responsible for what happens within creation.

A serious issue remains, however. Let's suppose that God is all-knowing, all-powerful, and all-good. Such a creator would know in advance all the choices people will make, the accomplishments and end results of their individual lives, as well as the overall destiny of humanity, from the beginning of time to the infinitely remote future. Such a creator would be able to change any of these eventualities in limitless numbers of ways. And this creator, being all-good, would want the best for every human being and for humanity as a whole. So whatever God "ordains," "lets be," or "makes to be" looks like something fixed and fated for all time, as an expression of God's very nature. Nor does it matter whether God exists within or outside of time, since all of the same attributes pertain to the deity in either case, and hence, the saga of humanity is set by divine creative choice at some original point. It would seem, then, that

God is responsible for whatever outcomes we find in the actual created universe. That being the case, there appears to be no difference between *this* framework of understanding and fatalism, since a relentless, inscrutable principle presides over every action or event and determines its outcome.

The diverse outlooks on and debates over predestination we have reviewed run parallel to power struggles in both sacred and political spheres across different parts of the world. But they have played a large role as well in bonding the faithful to their respective religions and maintaining their subservience to religious leaders (the official interpreters of doctrine). They have also helped shape both nonviolent forms of competition and robust campaigns of conquest for centuries.

Various religious denominations have also seen fit to condemn outsiders – those ignorant of their particular faith – to inevitable eternal punishment. Others, however, contend that special consideration is divinely extended to such blameless innocents. The underlying theological problem here (known as "the fate of the unlearned" or "the destiny of the unevangelized"[38]) revolves around the question of whether those who pre-existed the arrival of a certain prophet or divine messenger can nevertheless achieve salvation (retroactively, by proxy, or by some other means) at any time up to and including the day on which the deity delivers a final judgment on humanity. While most attention has been focused on those who are or were, through no fault of their own, ignorant of the faith's essential tenets (pagans, heathens, infants, and young children), an additional class of people is also of concern. This includes those who are aware of the faith's essential tenets to some degree or other, but are unwilling to embrace them (secularists, skeptics, agnostics, dilatory individuals, fence-sitters, inconsistent adherents), and those who are aware of but unacceptably modify or reject essential tenets of the faith (heretics, atheists, apostates). Whether salvation or condemnation is to be delivered to any of these is the fate univocally pronounced by certain influential religious spokespersons.

Inevitability, Persuasion, and Transhistorical Vision

Strong and persuasive rhetoric, particularly when it has predictive force, is capable of making things happen (as when we say a charismatic orator's fiery speech causes an insurrection), or at least of helping them to occur or failing to contribute to their prevention. There is no scientific research that explains with any certainty whether tabloid headlines like "Is War between the US and China Inevitable?" contribute to the occurrence of such devastating events. But it seems plausible that repeated verbal snapshots of possible historical futures like this accustom people to an idea and may therefore actually help precipitate the unthinkable.

Much of the discussion concerning climate change today revolves around evaluating whether humankind has sealed its own fate, having reached the "tipping point" of no return, after which catastrophic alteration of the planet is bound to happen. Many appeals and calculations focus on the amount of average temperature increase that the biosphere can tolerate before ecosystems become locked into a state of irreversible collapse. The jury remains out on whether there is any form of rhetoric that can scare self-interested humans into living in harmony with nature rather than seeking domination over it. Just as likely, it seems, is that many of us will hover in a state of inaction, dominated by a new form of mental paralysis known as "eco-anxiety" or "chronic fear of ecological doom."[39]

Two books on the outlook for earth's oceans link this struggle with the concept of fate: *The Ocean of Life: The Fate of Man and the Sea* and *The World Is Blue: How Our Fate and the Ocean's Are One*.[40] And another focuses on the land-based food crisis that is looming: *The Fate of Food: What We'll Eat in a Bigger, Hotter, Smarter World*.[41] Yet another calls for wholesale cutbacks to human consumption and the exploitation of nature: *An Inconvenient Apocalypse: Environmental Collapse, Climate Crisis and the Fate of Humanity*.[42] Is the demise of the biosphere something we can avert, or a passing horror show we can only observe with resignation? No one knows for sure. But certainly, belief that some cataclysmic threshold may have been crossed encourages many to give up hope. From this perspective, writer Richard Flanagan ponders whether the diminishing population of birds represents a "destiny" that is "perhaps only our postponed future" and is therefore a harbinger of humans' own demise.[43]

Recently, a group of researchers, led by historian Dagomar Degroot of Georgetown University, has urged that the story of past civilizations, featuring (among other factors) collapse in the wake of climate change, needs to be rewritten. This narrative, Degroot argues, overlooks the resourcefulness of societies, which through the past two millennia have often responded to environmental crises by developing new trade routes, cultivating different crops, changing their diets, practicing greater cooperation with others, applying better technologies, and discovering other adaptations to survive. This is not to deny that climate change is a real and serious factor in the decline and collapse of civilizations, but rather to suggest that human resourcefulness, creative thinking, and a willingness to break away from self-destructive behaviours and explore novel solutions can lead to greater resilience, improved social equality, and more sustainable lifestyles. These ideas are offered in the spirit of empowerment, to combat "Doomism" – the belief that humans are helplessly facing environmental calamity.[44] Another current report, from the Institute for Public Policy Research and Chatham House in the UK, similarly cites the risk of people worldwide falling into a climate change "doom loop" of self-reinforcing negativism that blocks them from finding solutions.[45]

Novelist Tim Winton, a longtime eco-activist, likewise speaks out against the despairing attitude of fateful acquiescence he thinks is gripping people in the face of declining environmental quality. This, he says, is happening because "those who lead us are … training citizens to accept the prospect of inexorable loss, unstoppable chaos, certain doom."[46] But why would our leaders do that? The "kinder" answer is that they themselves are ignorant, obstinate, and shortsighted. The less kind, or "deeper," analysis might be that they are greedily looking after their own and their cronies' narrow interests, and therefore acting to control the body politic in order to selfishly reap profits before the natural world collapses and the economy with it. Some wealthy leaders and their allies appear to think they can buy their way out of any crisis, as they are accustomed to doing. Whichever analysis one chooses, it seems that fate will have its day unless a vast majority of people come to their senses and rebel against having the future stolen from themselves and their children.

Living in the present moment has its unique challenges, among which can be counted the need to rise above the mentality of defeatism and victimization in order to overcome learned helplessness. In the coronavirus era, these challenges are compounded by the media. We've been told over and over, for example, that "the fate of many millions of people rests on … a vaccine for Covid-19 – the only sure escape route from the pandemic."[47] Thus, we are encouraged to think of ourselves as totally (and fatefully) dependent on medical intervention for a healthier future. But we could think of ourselves instead as creative, assertive beings who can change the world in positive, far-reaching ways – such as repairing our damaged relationship with the biosphere, which many scientists see as the ultimate cause of pandemics. (See also Afterword [I], "Fate in the Time of Pandemic.")

A Perspective on History

History may be understood both synchronically (in terms of events of the moment) and diachronically (as a product of long-term trends). And arguably both approaches are needed to gain as complete a picture as possible. Fate generally enters historical accounts in relation to forces that have been building up for a while, but these narratives may also reference fateful interventions and occurrences of a more isolated sort. Many historians grapple with fate either overtly or by implication, and their findings are often enigmatic. Vasily Grossman's book *Life and Fate*, for instance, presents "an epic tale of World War II and a profound reckoning with the dark forces that dominated the twentieth century."[48] Martin Meredith, in *The Fate of Africa*, argues that decisions, policies, choices, and mass movements have large-scale consequences and create institutions and events that seem beyond human control or influence. These lead to outcomes that large groups of people are left to confront and deal with as best they can.[49] Meredith raises here the problem of historical momentum and the ongoing reverberations it causes through time. There seems to be something to this conception, but it is exceedingly difficult to sort through. Do the energies of history (if we may call them that) truly surpass humans' ability to prevent their impact or to choose a different direction? Michael Holt, contends, for example, in *The Fate of Their Country*, that the American Civil War was the result of politicians' self-serving decisions. This suggests that it was not "inevitable," as some claim. But then he also posits, ambiguously, that in pursuing their separate agendas leaders of the time were "inexorably dragging the nation towards disunion," creating a state of affairs that was impossible to stop or alter.[50] Politicians often say they "had no other choice" except to do what they did, and historians may buy into this excuse. But it is no doubt more of a rationalization than a truthful testimony. Or so one hopes. For don't people always have *some* choice?

Progress and National Destiny

The Western world's preoccupation (or perhaps obsession) with progress yields one of the best illustrations of fatalism dressed up in the guise of historical inevitability. The ideal of human progress – from primitive beginnings to advanced modern civilization – became a foundational myth that united theories about social evolution with the desire (and obligation) to lift "unenlightened" peoples out of their state of ignorance and set them on the path to truth, godliness, and material success. Some have framed anthropological evidence from the past as showing that the genus *Homo sapiens* rose from its least perfect representatives to the "superior" exemplars of today. This translates into the story of progress which, unsurprisingly, doesn't have much of a future goal other than more widespread acquisition of the knowledge, consumer goods, comforts, and lifestyles already obtained by those lucky enough to live in the more advanced "First World."

Philosopher John Gray, in agreement with many historians, asserts that "Belief in progress is a relic of the Christian view of history as a universal narrative."[51] This narrative is closely linked with the notion of historical inevitability discussed earlier. Some of the major nineteenth-century European philosophers played an important part in cementing the idea of historical inevitability, including G.W.F. Hegel (1770–1831), Auguste Comte (1798–1857), and Karl Marx (1818–1883). Hegel believes that self-conscious reason will eventually triumph over unreason in human affairs. Reason, or rationality, has always been an integral driving force of history, but when it comes into its own, he argues, the Christian vision of God's work in the world will be realized, bringing with it an ideal form of political structure. Comte, often considered to be the founder of sociology and positivistic philosophy of science, holds that humanity moves through successive stages of thought about the world, from infantile supplication, to deities, to a mature scientific outlook that focuses on gathering knowledge and bettering the human condition. Marx, an atheist, nonetheless appropriates Hegelian thought to show how history follows a determinate path. While the conditions under which goods are produced depend upon the accumulation of wealth and the exploitation of labour, the laws of economics will eventually create developments that blossom forth into a world of social equality and a golden age of human flourishing. You can be sure that anyone who posits "laws" of historical stages is talking about fate rather than science – whatever might be said to the contrary.

Faith in "Divine Providence" has traditionally been a central pillar of the progressivist ideology. This is a way of looking at past and present established by those who have arrogated to themselves the right to articulate the meaning of history, and to impose their own parochial perspective on everyone.[52] Progressivist ideology reveals itself clearly via belief in the singular role of a nation (or group of nations). George Washington (1732–1799), for instance, proclaimed during the American Revolution that "The fate of unborn millions will now depend, under God, on the courage and conduct of this army" – meaning the one commanded by himself.[53] Poet Henry Wadsworth Longfellow (1807–1882) immortalized this revolutionary spirit in his famous telling of Paul Revere's midnight ride to warn patriots of the British army's movements, and, like Washington before him, couldn't resist an overblown narrative of the event, intoning that "the fate of a nation was riding that night."[54]

In the nineteenth century, Americans cited their "manifest destiny," first to justify expansionism across the continent, which displaced Native Peoples and Mexicans, and later to rationalize interference and military intervention overseas. These roles were thought to be divinely ordained duties; but the basic idea has since been transformed into the secular view known as "American exceptionalism." Similar bogus concepts have sprung up elsewhere, of course. As Bruce Pascoe argues in his far-reaching reappraisal of Australian Aboriginal history, at the time of British occupancy of Australia (starting with the First Fleet in 1788), "Europe was convinced that its superiority in science, economy, and religion directed its destiny. In particular, the British believed that their success in industry accorded their colonial ambition a natural authority, and that it was their duty to spread their version of civilisation and the word of God to heathens. In return, they would capture the wealth of the colonised lands."[55] Here, we have examples of naked self-aggrandizement disguised as destiny. Meanwhile, imperialistic adventurism cloaks itself in a moral imperative, grounded in a still higher metaphysical outlook. Nearly two centuries on, Charles de Gaulle (1890–1970), wartime hero and later President of France, affirmed, "Yes, it is Europe, from the Atlantic to the Urals, it is Europe, it is the whole of Europe, that will decide the fate of the world."[56] We can call this grandstanding, pompous perspective on human affairs *destiny politics*. Most noteworthy for our discussion, the phrase "national destiny" is a call to grab the bull by the horns, to consciously decide to act as a vehicle for realizing the state of affairs that *must be*. And here we find fate not only personified as the decisive historical energy of the moment or the arm of God – on horseback and on the battlefield – but also mapped onto the world as the intentional significance and deeper meaning of people's collective behaviour.

In times of war and in various violent movements aimed at influencing the course of history, fatalistic beliefs (including notions of genetic superiority to the enemy) have played a major role. Ideologies of warfare and conquest, as Kees Bolle points out, regularly feature "a notion of destiny … supposedly far beyond the value of individual lives. Well known are the endeavors to inculcate soldiers in the Nazi years in Germany with fatalism – in the dubious certainty that this was an ancient Germanic warrior stance."[57] As he goes on to observe, "cults of fate can revive much more easily than one may imagine." We see truth of this remark manifested in the constant flow of terrorist missions propelled by blind faith in ideals and allegedly preordained states of the nation or of the universe for which suicidal self-sacrifice is deemed obligatory. Ironically, both the perpetrators of these acts and their victims are in thrall to fate. Although it isn't easy or perhaps even possible to state who, or which forces, form and manipulate "cults of fate" (like those that embrace white supremacy or religious apocalypse), they nevertheless reveal both immediate and more remote and abstract kinds of social control at work. Pressures, threats, and conditioning (including brainwashing) create and reinforce internal conformity in such groups and fear of deviance from their norms. And the acts performed by group members against perceived outsiders may spread apprehension while locking both perpetrators and their victims into rigid roles they would not otherwise have chosen.

In Brief …

We have been looking at fate as a tool people use, cloaked behind one mask or another, in order to manipulate and control their fellow human beings, and have found many examples of fateful kinds of thinking that shut down individual freedom and autonomy. These range widely and include enduring sociopolitical trends (sex-based discrimination, racism, caste consciousness, genetic stereotyping); religious belief sets (divine control of reality, predestination); self-fulfilling prophecies (varieties of "doomism"); and political self-aggrandizement (belief in historic missions and national destinies). And perhaps we've learned to appreciate that our fate as individuals is – more often than we'd like to believe or admit – the product of what others do to or inflict upon us.

In Sebastian Barry's novel *The Temporary Gentleman* one character struggles against this reality with the succinct plea "Remember me, forget my fate."[58] This seems a fitting reminder that no matter how much other people seek to control us, or how much circumstances threaten to rule our destinies, there is hope beyond the limitations found within human life. For as we shall discover in the next chapter, many do take ownership of their fate even under the worst conditions, and many more do so through positive forms of self-assertion in the face of adversity. These acts affirm that what counts the most for us, whatever the odds may be, is the preservation of our personal identity, sense of worth, and sense of empowerment.

6

ATTITUDES TOWARD LIFE

A man's character is his fate.
– Heraclitus[1]

For me, I am the mistress of my fate …
– Shakespeare[2]

If life gives you lemons, make lemonade.
– Anonymous[3]

The Answer to Our Central Question

So in the end, who (or what) is in charge of human life: fate or ourselves as autonomous individuals? The short answer is: *we are in charge of our own lives.* This perspective, in contrast to the one examined in chapter 5, leads toward the active, positive, liberating aspect of choice, and of fate itself. The assumption underlying this "short answer" is and must be that "we" refers to people whose lives are not totally crushed by oppression of one kind or another, or by war, severe disease, congenital disorder, handicap, extreme addiction, total impoverishment, or some other dehumanizing, unavoidable, controlling set of circumstances. Let's pause for a moment to note that even persons who live under systems of oppression or who suffer serious, incurable illnesses, for example, can still take responsibility for their situation in various ways. They can flee from or oppose systems that enslave them, and/or assert themselves in spite of their ailments or misfortunes. And many do. It's easy to romanticize this possibility when considering it only in the abstract. Yet some exceptional individuals (such as Helen Keller [1880–1968], Stephen Hawking, and paralympic and world champion athletes like Australian tennis player Dylan Alcott) bravely transcend their limiting conditions, and go forward to lead lives of astonishing accomplishment. Our focus here is mainly on ordinary people whose lives and agency are not completely closed down by fateful factors, and whose narratives unfold under conditions that allow, at least in principle, for deliberation and choice. But what both extraordinary and ordinary individuals who are in charge of themselves have in common is the will to build a constructive form of life in the face of its given elements, and to strive to triumph over adversity.

A few considerations remain to be reviewed before we can rest content with the characterization just given. Fatefulness undeniably grounds human existence, as we've seen in previous chapters. And yet many thoughtful, creative, and meaningful responses to the presence of fate in human life are possible. Before we get to these, let's recall what we've discovered thus far about fate. Fortuitous factors – such as time and place of birth and death, "race," sex, and ethnicity, as well as the relentless condition of aging – shape the framework of each life, as do elements such as poverty or privilege, intelligence, and inborn talent. Special acts of fate enter unbidden into our personal existence periodically as well. Everyone constructs some kind of outlook on life and the world that aims to give overall sense to things, to account for why they aren't always under our control and don't fully make sense or conform to our expectations. In this context, theologian Helmer Ringgren comments that "Things happen to [us], they come upon [us], so to speak, from the outside … It is to this part of [our] existence that [we have] to get into some kind of relationship."[4] Our general perception of how we and others fare also raises questions about the justification of what takes place in the world, both near to and far from us. Michael Gelven observes that many people are likely to reflect on "why ... unearned fortune, either good or bad, happen[s] to *me*," why it happens to *anyone*, and then to ponder what such occurrences tell us about the nature of human existence in general.[5] These perspectives help identify the points where ideas about fate perennially enter the picture and begin to occupy our thoughts.

But beyond these somewhat philosophical moments, it is easily seen that even at a very basic level, the conduct of everyday life is continuously fateful. We get up in the morning, at some point we leave home and go outside, where we enter the flow of passing events in a world that is mostly oblivious to our existence and heedless of our public or private presence, having its own momentum and patterns that carry on largely unknown to and independent of us. Sometimes we have occasion to ponder that if we had been up a fraction earlier or later and entered this flow at a different interval, we might have discovered a moment of complete and blissful tranquility, or been caught up in a street celebration, a demonstration, a tragic event, or even a historically significant moment. An instant earlier or later and we might have been run over on the road, rescued from the road by a stranger, or able to rescue that same stranger from being run over. We enter daily life much as we would a rushing stream, which also has its own self-sustained temporal rhythm of passage. Novelist Amor Towles reflects, about a pair of his characters, that "the two young men hardly seemed fated for friendship. But Fate would not have the reputation it has if it simply did what it seemed it would do."[6] In other words, fate hands us outcomes that we would never expect or dream of, and often in backhanded or convoluted ways. Everyday existence includes these opaque moments or fateful junctures (which some would simply attribute to "chance"), that represent both arbitrary forks in the road and the unleashing of many influences upon us that we've had no foreknowledge of, and over which we have no control going forward. When things go wrong, we tend to think fate has disfavoured us ("Oh, fate must have frowned on me"), and when they go well, we don't think of fate at all. When someone miraculously or fortuitously survives a catastrophe, we joyfully celebrate; for those who perish we have pity but no answer to explain their having been singled out. For fate, we may say or think, is equally at work in either case.

Discussion in this book has mostly concerned fate as an individual phenomenon, that is, as it pertains to, shapes, or controls a single person's life. But we have also seen (for example, in chapter 5) that fate can be shared collectively, by an entire group at a certain historical moment or even over an extended period of time. Also, fate can and often does bind us to another person whose life has become entwined with our own, as when we develop a strong friendship or love-bond with someone. We take on the risk (or benefit) of a joint fate as the relationship grows and becomes more organic. Novelist Heather Rose calls our attention to this reality when one of her characters laments his wife's decision to cut him off from visiting her in a nursing home as her mental powers deteriorate: "It was tragic to lose her, but it would have been more tragic for them both to be prisoners to the one fate."[7] But although avoiding imprisonment to a joint fate may sometimes be possible, coming under its influence cannot always be averted. It may then become part of life's baggage that a person carries forward through the years.

These observations teach us that *cultivating a thoughtful attitude toward the inevitable is one of life's primary purposes and tasks.* If people held that the universe simply began without a cause – or at any rate without an intelligent deity as its cause – it would probably never have occurred to anyone that there might be such a thing as fate. For if all events were believed to result from the operation of natural laws plus chance factors, there would seem to be no gaps left over in the explanation of events, no room for supposing that fate decrees, determines, or produces anything. But if, on the other hand, fate signifies things that happen unpredictably and may be to our major advantage or detriment – whether decreed by a superpower, originating mysteriously, or emerging from within the core of choices we have made – the role we assign to this concept within our perception of reality then becomes quite important. There are doubtless many ways in which a fateful thought process develops. But as we shall see shortly, striking episodes of personal experience and instructive tales or legends present some of the primary avenues for arriving at and reconciling oneself with fateful beliefs.

We can now ask where philosophical persuasion fits into the whole picture of fateful belief. As we saw in chapter 4, this is a somewhat vexed question, inasmuch as logical arguments appeal to some but leave others cold. In this connection, Helena Eilstein poses an interesting question: "Why does the acceptance of fatalism *on the metaphysical level of thinking* typically matter so little in the practical life of its supporters?"[8] That is, she queries why there is a disconnection between the way people either affirm or deny fate in their everyday lives, on the one hand, and the case that is made for fatalism as a theory about ultimate reality, on the other. The answer to Eilstein's question isn't clear. Most people who accept that fate influences their lives are persuaded in this direction by considerations other than the forcefulness of philosophers' abstract reasoning or any beliefs about the nature of things. But it would be wrong to conclude that careful reflection – on fate and many other things besides – plays little or no part in the process of belief formation about fate. Many examples in this book have proven otherwise. When we think about the human condition, we must also realize that ignorance resides at the heart of our outlook on the world, and that it's wise to accept this fact in framing whatever we say and do. Since fate is called upon to fill the gaps where we cannot hope to find answers or explanations, part of this acceptance may be called "learning to live with fate," "integrating fate with other aspects of life," or "taking hold of fate." But once again, perhaps the most important lesson we learn from contemplating fate is that we don't have to be fatalists to believe in fate (see chapter 1). Fate plays a significant, sometimes even crucial part in our lives;

however, it does not control everything we do; it does not rule the universe. Or at least we have found no compelling reason to think so. (It is probably easier to fall into the trap of thinking about fate as all-controlling when it is personified, as in ancient Greece – an approach we have deliberately avoided in this book.)

We believe our activities are *mostly* under our own control, products of choice, and we have good reasons for thinking so. Well, then, how should we learn to live affirmatively with fate? There is no operating manual for the successful conduct of a fateful life; but those who wish to reach this goal can appropriate ideas from a number of sources that may prove useful. Traditional narratives about exemplary figures who've been challenged by fate and have somehow triumphed provide one important paradigm. We will call the subjects of these tales *heroes of fate* because they have resolutely taken a stand before the unknown and/or unyielding forces that govern their lives. Let's examine how such courage helps us make sense of things.

Heroes of Fate

How often do we hear others say that some unresolved situation or future possibility rests "in the hands of fate"? How often do we find ourselves making such statements? Probably more frequently than we realize. Especially when life is looking a bit grim or beyond our control, that's the time we are most likely to invoke the idea of fate. "Just what you might expect from life," we reflect, "sorrows are dished out randomly, and you never know what's coming your way." But we also call on fate – as indeed people before us have always done – when we consider how the world itself is going. Well, how is it going? "It's going to hell in a handbasket" is a facetious response one sometimes hears. This is only a colourful expression of the judgment that things are in an inevitable downward spiral toward some cataclysmic or apocalyptic finish, a self-destructive endpoint. The entire cosmos, it may be held, is likewise stuck in a gargantuan handbasket – doomed to suffer some ultimate, incomprehensible process of self-annihilation.

However, fate has its bright side too. For example, someone might say, "It was totally unlikely that we'd ever meet again, but fate brought us together, and here we are. And we've lived happily ever after." A lovely tale, to be sure, centring on an outcome apparently dictated for those involved by the enigmatic workings of the world. Think also for a moment of those individuals who affirm or discover their fate and then courageously resolve to embrace it. We might be tempted to say that this commitment amounts to an illusory piece of behaviour, or is an unfree act or piece of deceptive disavowal of responsibility. But perhaps it's not. People can, of course, fall very readily into a pattern of feeling sorry for themselves, uselessly railing against their lot in life and finding excuses for their own dilatory conduct. Yet they also often decide to take hold of their situation and run with it. It has been observed that there are basically three kinds of attitudes toward fate: resignation, futile resistance, and heroic acceptance.[9] The last of these types – which has animated much great literature – is by far the most interesting, because it elevates creative resolve and self-assertion to a place of prominence. And perhaps "heroic acceptance" doesn't quite do justice to those cases in which fate is dynamically embraced. Giuseppe Faggin observes that "one may say: 'Follow your destiny, fulfill your destiny', but not, 'Follow your fate.'"[10] The matter is not that simple, however, because transforming fate is a viable and meaningful option. A few examples will illustrate the point.

On the twentieth anniversary of 9/11, a significant essay appeared in *Esquire* magazine on the ethics and meaning of photographing and publishing images of people who took their own lives by jumping or falling from the World Trade Center twin towers on the day of the terrorist attack that destroyed these New York (and American) landmarks.[11] The author's initial assertion is that "the Falling Man" who was depicted in the piece didn't choose his fate but seized it anyway.

This is meant to indicate that *even within the scope of an inevitability, a free person can still nonetheless choose among ways (or enact a particular way) of facing it and appropriating the critical moment.*

The same theme resonates within the plots of many classical and didactic tales. In Sophocles' play *Antigone* (441 BCE or earlier), the title character affirms her fate through the principled action she clings to, despite the tragic consequences for herself of doing so. King Creon of Thebes has forbidden Antigone to bury her brother Polyneices because of his role in the civil war that has led to Polyneices' death and Creon's ascent to the throne. Antigone defies Creon, out of a desire to honour her family and respect the gods with a proper burial. In so doing, she embraces her own fateful demise, and indeed actualizes it herself by committing suicide – an ultimate, if paradoxical, act of self-assertion.

The *Bhagavad Gita*, part of the Hindu sacred scripture known as the *Mahabharata* (written down about 400 CE, though originating from much earlier), tells how the warrior Arjuna had revealed to him by the god Krishna a mighty vision of the world's fate and of his own role in the final battle that will end in universal destruction. After wrestling with himself over his conflicting duties (since some of his enemies will be his own kin), Arjuna commits himself to fight, thus willingly carrying out his fate. Antigone and Arjuna are much-celebrated icons of the history of fate and there are many others in the literature and mythology of nations and cultures across the globe, most of whom are less well-known, as the next two examples illustrate.

Claudius (10 BCE–54 CE), the Roman emperor who ruled during the period between Caligula and Nero, was allegedly a beneficiary of empowering omens and is another (if unlikely) hero of fate. An awkward and sickly child and the butt of much public ridicule (including by his own mother), he was nonetheless appointed consul as a young man by Caligula. According to the historian Suetonius (69–103/140 CE), on Claudius' first entry into the Forum in this new role, an eagle flew to him and sat on his shoulder – a portent of his future ascent to power. Later, when he became emperor and the target of would-be assassins, eagles symbolically returned to his rescue. On this second occasion, military standards (rods with replica eagles at the top end, considered sacred and ceremonially driven into the ground) proved impossible to be removed and carried into battle. Claudius' army interpreted this as a divinely given sign that they were to stay in Dalmatia and remain loyal to Claudius. They thus turned on his rival Scribonianus and sent him fleeing for his life.[12]

Albert Camus (1913–1960), in *The Myth of Sisyphus*, reconstructs the mythological character who – for his transgressions that include attempting to cheat Death, insubordination to the gods, and general hubris – was condemned by Zeus to endlessly repeat the task of rolling a boulder up a hill, only to find it rolling back down again, out of his control. This absurd situation strikes Camus' fancy, and serves, he thinks, as an instructive example for all of us: "At each of those moments when [Sisyphus] leaves the heights and gradually sinks toward the lairs of the gods, he is superior to his fate. He is stronger than his rock." Sisyphus is conscious and therefore also free. And so he can adopt a self-saving attitude of triumph over his circumstances: "There is no fate that cannot be surmounted by scorn," Camus declares. Camus projects onto this archetypal figure a kind of contentment because "His fate belongs to him. His rock is his thing ... The struggle itself toward the heights is enough to fill a man's heart. One must imagine Sisyphus happy."[13] Camus thus urges his readers to imagine that in relation to one's fate it is the ongoing process of resistance and performance that matters, not the ultimate outcome.

Unfortunately, Camus veers away from defiance of fate when it comes to the subject of death, as we see intimated when he writes: "If there is a personal fate, there is no higher destiny, or at least there is but one which [Sisyphus] concludes is inevitable and despicable. For the rest, he knows himself to be the master of his days."[14] The questionable claim embedded here appears to be that death is that singular aspect of fate toward which any resolute, self-affirming stance is futile. But is it? We will return to this issue in a moment.

Cataclysmic Scenarios

Besides the titanic struggles of fateful heroes, there are numerous stories of supreme clashes at the end of the universe. Norse mythology envisions a staggering, cosmos-shattering battle known as Ragnarok. The god Odin has sequestered an elite band of warriors in the afterlife paradise of Valhalla, awaiting this showdown. Nevertheless, both humans and gods – plus all of creation – are doomed to perish in a monumental clash with a race of giants. This epic struggle and fatalistic outcome resonates with Christian myths of Armageddon, the opening of the Seven Seals of God, the Apocalypse, and the Last Judgment, but also with the tale of Arjuna summarized earlier. Even more remarkably, it jibes with more modern scientific ideas positing the freeze-death of the universe, or its collapse or shredding by dark matter, or some other radical transformation.[15] Author Daniel McCoy asserts, however, that to the Viking mind "the tale didn't produce hopelessness as much as inspiration and invigoration. Just as the gods will one day die, so too will each individual human being. And just as the gods will go out and face their fate with dignity, honor, and courage, so too can humans. In this view, the inevitability of death and misfortune should not paralyze us, but should instead spur us to hold noble attitudes and do noble deeds."[16] So even within a worldview that foretells its own finality, there can be hope and a motivation to accomplishment and self-distinction.

The cosmic battle theme also appears in Zoroastrianism (founded in ancient Persia, around 1,200–1,000 BCE). The deity Ahura Mazda is engaged in a cataclysmic battle with evil spirit Ahriman for control of the universe. Good eventually triumphs over evil in the ultimate fate of the world, as in other belief systems and narratives. But fate inheres in the timespan of the cosmos: when time expires, a final judgment is rendered on all that exists. This outlook strongly influenced Manichaeism as well as Gnostic and other early mainstream Christian thinking,[17] and it forms part of the cultural background to Islam as well. In addition to a correspondence with Norse mythology, there is an interesting parallel here with Hinduism, for at the battle where Arjuna comes face to face with the Supreme Lord Krishna (see chapter 2), the deity proclaims, "Time I am, the mighty destroyer of worlds, and I come to vanquish all living beings."[18] It is not difficult to identify with this notion of time as an inexorable force, since we experience it this way in our daily lives. But a special meaning attaches to time in many of the exemplary tales we have been looking at, namely, the sense in which "time runs out" at a certain (fateful) point – where endgames run their course and final judgments are rendered.

Birth

Whatever one might think of fate as a phenomenon and of fatalism as a philosophical commitment, there remain two basic parameters of life that set boundaries we cannot alter: the points of birth and death. These therefore seem to be the best candidates for viewing fate at work. Much effort is expended by individual humans in either adjusting to or recontextualizing the facts of their own birth, which is an unprecedented, involuntary, perplexing event.[19] Birth, the beginning of one's proper existence, is the imponderable weight that we must bear and come to terms with during our lives. Gelven regards "the birthday celebrant" as one whose behaviour represents an outstanding symbolic affirmation of fate. He reasons that although a birth is "certainly caused and biologically explainable, [it] remains a mystery to the extent that who one *is* as a result of this event surpasses its explanatory power."[20] In other words, the astonishing fact of being born isn't reducible to just the fact of one's parents being fated to meet. It isn't only that a unique individual comes into life each time a birth takes place; rather, *that anyone at all does so* seems an extraordinary emergence into being – some kind of ontological miracle, as it were. Philosopher Martin Heidegger (1889–1976) colourfully suggests that the significance of birth is that humans are "thrown" into existence and then have to take responsibility for doing something about it, for taking the world as it is dished out, transforming it and one's own life in relation to it.[21] Thus, notwithstanding a fateful arrival on Earth, each individual must carve out a path through a lifelong series of valuations, choices, actions, and reactions. We do this by seizing the moment and making something of it (or not).

Death

Death is the other fixed point, whether one interprets it as the complete cessation of existence or as a threshold beyond which we pass into a different realm of being. The forms of death-denial in which people engage are, of course, quite numerous, from vicarious survival-against-the-odds while watching horror films or TV wilderness competitions; to cults of youth and cosmetic surgery; to cryogenics (corpse freezing); to triumphant flirtations with fatality in "death-defying" stunts and "extreme sports"; to belief in reincarnation. But much of human life is oriented in more empowering ways, which feature death-acknowledgment and recognition of our mortality. Hospice care, death preparedness and euthanasia groups, grieving, mourning, funerals, cremations, wakes, vigils, Day of the Dead celebrations, and diverse observances such as last rites, rites of passage, and rituals of remembrance and memorializing the dead, are all ways of confronting fate and actively taking charge of death. Belief in an afterlife – an essential element of most religions – can be seen as signifying both acts of coming to terms with fate in the form of death and assertions of victory over it.

Philosophers, theologians, and spiritual leaders of all stripes have perennially endorsed the idea that life is (largely or even entirely) a process of preparing for death and thus confronting our universal fate. This may entail cultivating a form of contemplation, a spiritual practice, a certain physical style of living, or some other disciplined kind of self-education and refinement. Socrates is said to have argued (in Plato's dialogue *Phaedo*[22]) that living properly is a matter of getting ready to die, which in turn involves developing the soul for the moment of its beatific release from "the prison of the body." Buddhism similarly teaches that learning how to approach death in an enlightened manner is of major importance to the living (see the eighth- century CE *Tibetan Book of the Dead*,[23] for example). This is because understanding death helps us to better appreciate the impermanence of all things and to place mortality in perspective, focus on making life more worthwhile, remove the fear of dying, and, by improving how we live, to obtain a good quality of rebirth. Resurrection (bodily or spiritual) is a central tenet of both Christianity and much earlier religions. Jesus' resurrection at Eastertime is loaded with embellishments of symbolic meaning, including hope for everyone's survival of death in some form. To the ancient Egyptians and Canaanites, Baal and Osiris were gods who die and achieve rebirth. As with other pre-Christian gods who undergo death and resurrection, they are associated with rejuvenation of nature and fecundity. Likewise, Inanna (or Ishtar), a Sumerian/Mesopotamian goddess, after dying in conflict with other supernatural beings, descends to the underworld and then returns, and the fallout from these events becomes the mythic cause of seasonal cycles. The Greeks' Persephone (Proserpine to the Romans) dies and becomes reborn as the goddess of spring, which has been equated with the renewal of life on Earth.

At the point of birth, there are many persons we might become during life, and, as we have seen, fate plays a significant role in determining which one(s) is (or are) realized by each of us. When we die, so too die all the persons we might have been or believe we could have been. This is the pool of unactualized potentials we possess, those characteristics we did not realize in order that we might manifest others instead. The narrator of one of Gerald Murnane's novels sums things up in this way: "Each year when I look around the cemetery at Fawkner I know I am looking at the place where all my lives, actual or conjectured, will end. Whoever I am, whoever I might otherwise have been, whoever I might yet become – the lives of all these men will end in the one grassland, only four kilometres from the street where I was born."[24] The way a life develops is a complex mixture of given conditions, choices, and acts of self-making, plus circumstances beyond our control that often have game-changing impacts and unexplainably appear out of the blue. Whatever may be the causal account of how such impacts unfold, these elements are still pieces of fate that use up our options to one extent or another.

Suicide

Some people choose suicide – so don't they, at least, know in advance (even if only a little ahead) what their cause of death will be, and thus pre-empt their fate to that extent? Well, maybe, except that not all attempted suicides are successful. Futhermore, other circumstances might befall someone who is contemplating ending it all. For instance, a rock or a shop front marquee might unpredictably fall on his head, or a hurricane might sweep through, killing him while he's still contemplating suicide.

Being genetically predisposed to suicidal ideation doesn't mean that you will actually die in this manner, either. If we say so-and-so committed suicide, and argue that this proves the person had a suicidal disposition all along, we beg the question by assuming that performing any act manifests a pre-existing tendency to do so, which explains in turn why the act occurred. But of course the proposed account doesn't explain anything. (Such pseudo-explanation, which goes around in a circle or lifts itself up by its own bootstraps – that the doing of X is caused by the "propensity to do X" – was satirized long ago by Molière [1622–1673] in his play *The Physician in Spite of Himself*.[25]) Perhaps some people *do* have a "suicidal nature," but this is a conclusion that needs to be independently established by investigation, not simply asserted after the fact as if it were self-evident. And in any case, having a certain trait does not necessarily entail an inability to override, control, or otherwise change it. To assume that we don't have this ability is again question-begging, since it implies that however we act is predetermined, and that nothing we do can alter or modify our basic life circumstances. But this needs to be shown, not just taken for granted.

Returning to the topic of suicide itself, however, it looks as if taking one's own life may have to be counted as yielding at least *some* exceptions to the rule that the time and place of one's death is fatefully set.

A Cautionary Lesson

The above example of begging the question indicates that we likewise need to avoid falling into the same trap when attributing events in general to fate. Why did Z happen? Someone might say, "because it was fated to happen," or simply: "It must have been fate." When challenged about why she said that, suppose the reply is that "Z was so overwhelmingly *unlikely* and yet occurred anyway, so it must have been *inevitable*." This sort of thinking is often concealed behind expressions like "It was (or was not) meant to be"; "Fate works in strange ways"; "It was going to take place, no matter what"; and so on. If we posit that fate is at work, then we must do so for good reasons and not owing to intellectual indolence and self-vindication. Yet regardless of what we think about fate things *are* sometimes out of our control, and events occur for reasons we cannot fathom, or for reasons that are mostly hidden from view. Consequently, although it is best to be cautious about invoking the idea of fate when seeking to explain what goes on in our lives, it still holds an important place in our overall view of the world.

Fateful Lives

There is a tendency to depict fated events as somehow extraordinary, when they often may be just among the many components of a life. From one perspective, most of our decisions can be seen, on the one hand, as causally efficacious – as contributing to future states of affairs – and, on the other hand, as fateful – in relation to the meaning they potentially give to our lives. Also, the choices we make create elements of fate, so to speak, because they most often cannot be unmade or reversed, given the direction of time as we live through it, as well as other complications surrounding events in the world. But this hardly entails that *every* fated outcome is noteworthy or portentous. Nonetheless, as we've discovered in previous chapters, some – and perhaps many – situations we find ourselves in do represent decisive existential moments. As Søren Kierkegaard (1813–1855) revealingly suggested, we all encounter "that fork on the road … where the path branches off."[26] While he stresses that he means a critical juncture at which we make a major choice, there is something about such a choice that is fateful as well, in that we can neither turn back nor turn away from it, and we cannot redo it, nor predict it or escape from its long-term consequences. (Even those images and utterances that have the power to radically change our lives cannot be "un-seen" or "un-heard" once we have been exposed to them.)

The idea that fate plays an important role in shaping our individual biographies sometimes leads to careless and overblown caricatures of human life itself. Should we nevertheless say that our lives are in some sense "ruled by fate"? If so, what would that mean for us? We've seen that not all conceptions of a fateful world are identical. A variety of fateful outlooks are possible and have been imagined or theorized, some more positive and energizing than others. There are ways of apprehending life that make it seem completely locked in by fate. Some individuals have willingly adopted this perspective because it relieves them of the burden of responsibility for their actions, or else readily fills gaps in their ability to explain the world, or fits in with a religious belief system that they already adhere to. Other viewpoints portray fate as just one force among many at work on us in our daily lives, all of which may even be in competition with each other. And within the domain of self-realization, the formative notion that a person can seize control of her own destiny remains appealing today, as we've seen. This seems to reinforce the view that destiny, though often equated with fate, is nonetheless a different concept (see chapter 1). The discrepancy between statements about destiny and fate may derive from the way in which fate inclines us to think of what has already happened or is inevitably going to happen, whereas destiny strikes us as embodying an intimated direction or promise that needs some essential agency, some push, to become actualized. However, we've also seen that *people can choose to actively take hold of their fate*, which signifies both a concept and a practice that move significantly beyond fate as something we merely follow.

A more objective reason for believing in fate is suggested by biology. Everyone carries a certain genetic inheritance that will almost certainly manifest itself, no matter what. Physical endowments – body type, general health profile, appearance – are (or largely are) unavoidable properties we possess from the get-go. As well, everyone will eventually die from some cause or other. But few of us know very far in advance what that cause will be. (For instance even a person with a terminal disease might die instead in a car accident or miraculously recover; and a prisoner on death row may be fatally stabbed or pardoned before being executed.) Our genetic inheritance may indicate that we have, say, a 75 per cent chance of dying from a certain disease. However, even for serious diseases that have no known cure or method of prevention, we might be lucky enough to belong in the 24.8 per cent that either won't die from them or the tiny 0.2 per cent that spontaneously recover or are saved by an obscure or novel treatment procedure or a placebo.

Our complex environmental, cultural, social, and historical emplacement – determined by the time and place of our birth – is a fixed matrix that some philosophers designate as the "facticity" of life.[27] This term refers collectively to the elements of givenness, the "brute facts," that existence calls on us individually to relate and respond to, as we become who we will be in the world. Some of us become capable and desirous of transcending our basic birth conditions, and others don't. Whether heredity or other influences "fate us" to have one or the other of these motivational sets is something we can never fully understand or predict. When all is said and done, the healthiest and most constructive view of being human assumes that (unless proved otherwise) *we have it within our power to choose a form of life; and the form we decide upon is a product of freedom acting upon givenness to creatively produce ourselves.*

Experiencing Fate

Sometimes fate is invoked to refer to a life situation that people sense themselves becoming imprisoned by, locked into, or defined by, as if drifting on an unforgiving current or tide into a place from which there is no escape. Thus, one character in Rachel Cusk's novel *Outline* "approached the prospect of the job in London with a reverse kind of fatalism, as though the very freedom of his life was something for which he was at last going to pay by going into harness."[28] After mothballing his much beloved boat in an urban storage shed, this character leaves Athens, and the book's omniscient narrator comments: "And then off he went to London, sensing that he himself was about to suffer much the same fate."[29] What this individual evidently fears is that he will assume the identity of a mere thing as he becomes stuck in a role where his life is circumscribed ever more closely by demands and expectations. In Dominic Smith's novel *The Electric Hotel*, a struggling, self-made movie producer envisions himself as "an ashcan tycoon … who couldn't outrun his own fate." And the protagonist, badly wounded while employed as a wartime cameraman, "saw his own reflection … and knew it was a kind of preparation, a moment of staring into his own fate."[30] The feeling that one is a puppet of circumstances and events, and of giving in to fate's inevitability is very strong in all these examples. Most of us can relate to this feeling from our own experience. And many will also no doubt be able to share the sense that fate sometimes catches up with us in its own sweet time.

A different sense of fate, however, may be garnered by those who feel its shadow as a kind of positive, value-laden inheritance. The story of Stan Grant, an Indigenous Australian journalist, political commentator, and author, provides an example. His biography illustrates how fate shapes the narrative of an entire family. Grant relates how members of the white Irish family that forms part of his ancestry were all condemned to death for a crime they had committed, and for which they were held jointly responsible. All except one. For reasons unknown, his great-grandfather's life was spared, and he was sent to the penal colony with which the British founded Australia. As Grant observes, "This is another one of those moments where fate intervenes and gives birth to an entirely new history. John Grant would be sent to New South Wales and bring his story and his name. It is the name I still carry."[31] Of course, Stan Grant would not even exist if this historic moment hadn't unfolded as it did. What was the missing reason why this event happened? A glitch in procedure? A clerical error? An arbitrary decision by someone in the background? A liberating act of favouritism? Without further information (which is not recorded anywhere), it's anyone's guess. If such information were available, it would enable Grant to complete the account of his great-grandfather's personal history and achieve a greater level of insight and understanding. Even so, it might remain a stark, unexplainable fact that this individual, John Grant, was singled out for special treatment. The givenness of John Grant's life, then, links up with that of Stan Grant's, perhaps more dramatically but no less definitively than that of each person's ancestry. (See also the discussion of shared fate earlier in this chapter, and of group fate in chapter 5.)

Many other real-life and apocryphal cases express the brute facticity and serendipity of circumstances that govern people's lives. But they may also be tinged by a touch of reprieve or deliverance. Consider the biblical figure of Barabbas. As related in all four Gospels, Barabbas, a known criminal and murderer, was the crowd's choice to be released from impending crucifixion instead of Jesus Christ, when

Roman governor Pontius Pilate asked the rabble to give a voice vote of preference for the customary act of mercy. While some might say that this was part of God's obscure plan, others might simply see it as fate intervening once again. Another interesting example comes from Armando Iannucci's 2017 political satire film *The Death of Stalin*. In one scene, after Josef Stalin (1879–1953) dies, Lavrentiy Beria (1899–1953), the deceased leader's real-life deputy premier and head of security and the secret police, manoeuvres for power by suddenly releasing political prisoners, just as they are about to be individually shot through the head. "Fate intervenes" at this moment, then, to spare the lives of the anonymous men lined up in a row against a wall, men who await their turn to be murdered by servants of the state. In a way, it doesn't matter whether these events really unfolded exactly as they have been depicted or rather are totally or largely fictional, so long as we understand the fateful lesson the stories teach. We have all heard about, and have perhaps even experienced, large or small-scale "rescues" of a comparably striking sort. It also doesn't matter whether we ourselves can give a causal explanation of such outcomes. No doubt there is one. Someone issued a directive or command that led to lives being spared by fearful and obedient minions of the state. "Why at this exact moment?" someone might ask. "That's just the way it happened," comes the reply. But "that's just the way things happen" is pretty much the hallmark of fateful occurrences.

Living with (or without) fate is a matter of whether and how people constitute their lives for good or ill. We might say that it is a matter of how they choose to build their lives (always remembering with humility, however, that whether we are ever free to choose *anything* is a question lurking in the dark heart of fatalism). The lives we lead are constructed as narratives; they are built up of tales we tell ourselves and others. These may be more or less comprehensive and intelligible, but there's no law stating that a story must be complete, make total sense, or be immune to revision. There are even those who maintain that the best ones are open-ended, that is, unfinished and ripe for further development, in imagination or in reality. What do all these stories mean, what do they tell us? One salient feature of fate is that it often *closes* stories or at least chapters of stories. A believer in fate may struggle against that fact or celebrate it, depending on how she is reconciled with the outcome in question. If a painful episode in someone's life is brought to a close, that's a good thing; if a quest for something very rewarding is cut short, that's a bad thing. And of course either of these eventualities might be ascribed to a twist of fate. Belief in fate or fatalism may be coöpted in the service of rationalizing the course of a life and therefore may appear, or be, disingenuous. Success and happiness (however conceived) may be attributed to "good fortune," "an act of grace," or related powers. But as Eilstein observes, it is also the case that "people sometimes try to find in fate an escape from a profound feeling of guilt or of responsibility for their failure to achieve a satisfactory life."[32] Fair enough. Yet perhaps there are more honest or at least more circumspect ways of affirming fatefulness in our lives and learning to live with it, as will now be explained.

Being True to Fate

The concept of "being true to fate" sounds a bit odd, but it does the job of embracing the many attitudes there are toward reconciling belief in fate and creating a satisfactory life for oneself. Retired actor and activist Michael J. Fox (no relation) gives concrete expression to this concept when reflecting on how Parkinson's disease and other misfortunes have necessitated reshaping his life: "Acceptance doesn't mean resignation. It means understanding that something is what it is and there's got to be a way through it."[33] We have looked at a wide range of creative responses to humans' fateful condition: the outlooks associated, for example, with the karma strand of Hinduism; Stoicism; Mongol culture; Chinese traditional thought; the worldview of the Omaha First Nation of America; the stances taken by "heroes of fate"; and more. An important addition to this list is Daoism (or

Taoism), the ancient Chinese philosophical/religious school of thought that, in a way, summarizes the core belief shared by all perspectives on the everyday world and the cosmos that are influenced by fatalism.

Daoism

According to Daoism's fundamental insight, whatever is or might be emerges from a single source of energy, being, and order. As its ancient canonical text (written between the eighth and third centuries BCE) affirms, "Tao [Dao] is beyond words/and beyond understanding./ Words may be used to speak of it,/but they cannot contain it ... Tao is a whirling emptiness,/yet when used it cannot be exhausted./Out of this mysterious well/flows everything in existence."[34] To live in harmony with this principle – the Dao or "the way" – is the path to fulfillment and virtue. The existential practice prescribed here is (in today's language) to "go with the flow." But as with other recipes of a similar sort, this advice is more easily uttered than understood and acted upon. It is generally agreed that "Dao" signifies two things: (a) the ultimate, unknowable, ineffable, eternally present, inexhaustible, and infinitely powerful shaping force of the universe; and (b) the manner in which all things grow and develop, decline and die, and express opposing tendencies and qualities. It follows that to take control of one's life and make it productive, one should strive to grasp how the Dao works and energizes the world, and act in accordance with this insight.

Stephen Bokenkamp interprets this precept as follows: "While all existence is seen to be part of the Dao, movements away from its primordial condition of unity are held to be destructive, evil, and transgressive. The perfect human is thus imagined to be a flawless microcosm of the cosmic whole, with the bodily spirits perfectly attuned to their counterparts in the macrocosm."[35] The central guideline here – shared with many other religious and philosophical doctrines – is that there is a transcendent reality governing everything that occurs in the world; one can either embrace and work with it (which is beneficial), or exist in conflict with it (which is detrimental and self-destructive). But there is very little distance between such views and the idea that fate rules our lives and must be a major reference-point for self-making.

Comprehensive theories of fate have always stipulated forms of conduct appropriate to conditions of existence that we cannot control and must learn to live with. To put the matter briefly, you can either go with the flow or go against the flow, but the flow will go its own way whatever you do; so to go against it means it will just roll over you or sweep past. This is roughly tantamount to saying that the secret of life is to discover what fate has in store for us, accept it, and act in harmony with it. Thus does East meet West; for this is also the essential message of ancient Roman Stoicism (see pages 37–9).

Nietzsche and Amor Fati

Friedrich Nietzsche (1844–1900) propounds an analogous doctrine that he calls "*amor fati*" ("love of fate"). As we have seen earlier in this chapter and in chapters 2 and 3, many thoughtful writers have taught that you should or must embrace your fate. Of course, you have to accept your fate. And you need to learn how to deal with it and carve out a life for yourself. But can anyone go beyond this and really *love* their fate if it is not a particularly happy one, or worse still, if it is tragic or horrible? Does it even make sense to talk this way? At first glance, the answer is no, and thus when discussing Nietzsche, there appear to be two alternatives: either he is talking nonsense or else a more subtle interpretation of his message must be sought. Nietzsche, although prone to making grandiose and bombastic claims, is actually a very careful and inspired thinker and writer, and consequently the benefit of the doubt should incline us toward the second approach. The concept of amor fati has been widely (and wildly) processed by the gristmill of scholarly analysis, but we needn't be drawn into this miasma of discourse. First let's see what he actually says, and then place this key idea into Nietzsche's overall philosophical project.

In *The Gay Science*, Nietzsche frames what is probably his best-known deliverance about amor fati, within the context of a New Year's resolution:

> Today everybody permits himself the expression of his wish and his dearest thought; hence I, too, shall say what it is that I wish from myself today, and what was the first thought to run across my heart this year – what thought shall be for me the reason, warranty, and sweetness of my life henceforth. I want to learn more and more to see as beautiful what is necessary in things; then I shall be one of those who make things beautiful. *Amor fati*: let that be my love henceforth! I do not want to wage war against what is ugly. I do not want to accuse; I do not even want to accuse those who accuse. Looking away shall be my only negation. And all in all and on the whole: some day I wish to be only a Yes-sayer![36]

This scarcely sounds like the ravings of a madman or fool. But before we can grasp his words with any accuracy, a brief look at Nietzsche's general outlook is essential.

Nietzsche's complex philosophy should be understood as a form of cultural revisionism, that is, as an attempt to revitalize or re-energize human life in the wake of what he calls "the death of God."[37] He believes, for various reasons, that Judeo-Christian thinking and values have run their course and have ceased to provide inspiration for human achievement and excellence. In particular, Nietzsche maintains that Christianity (at least as an organized religion) has always been based upon the mistake of exalting suffering, weakness, and death. It also, by his reckoning, promotes a general outlook of negativism, nihilism, defeatism, and world-weariness, which he identifies as varieties of "nay-saying" to life. Using an astonishing number of rebellious thought experiments, Nietzsche aims to liberate people from existential subservience to ways of living that have ultimately failed to maximize humans' potential for becoming creative, assertive, and self-sufficient beings. By means of a vast deconstructive critique of the entire Western cultural heritage, he attempts to show how humans could be freed from bondage to the past, in order to be free for embarking on new and fresh adventures in response to the challenges of the future. In short, he wants to shake up all of our cherished notions about ourselves and the world around us, and to instigate a revolution in values.

Against this background, we can see that in the passage from *The Gay Science* quoted above, Nietzsche advocates (albeit only for himself) the idea of leading a more positive and constructive life. This is one that makes better use of energy and creativity, and that, by adopting an affirmative and resolute viewpoint, enables a better person to evolve. The goal is a kind of individual who says "yes" to life as a whole, including all of its highs and lows, its blessings, limitations, and drawbacks. Nietzsche's prescription is that we commit ourselves to live, in the face of those things that cannot be changed, *as if we had willed them* and not be bogged down by regrets, false hopes, and feelings of failure and self-loathing. Let us suppose, he says, that it's as if we had wished for everything to happen just as it does in fact happen. He wants us to put ourselves to the test in response to his thought, and see what we are made of.

Elsewhere in his writing, Nietzsche observes, "It is part of this state [amor fati] to perceive not merely the necessity of those sides of existence hitherto denied, but their desirability … for their own sake, as the more powerful, more fruitful, truer sides of existence, in which its will finds clearer expression."[38] Can you take a dare? Can you cast away your mental and emotional crutches? Can you live with passionate intensity and unflagging optimism? Can you go where no one else has gone? Can you "become what you are"?[39] Questions like these come up regularly in the literature of today's self-help movement, but it is arguable that Nietzsche pioneers such ideas, as he challenges us to discover and tap into our inner strengths.[40]

Now let's return to the question whether we can realistically embrace fate with open arms and joyful resolve. Is this just an extreme view that has nothing of value to offer ordinary mortals? If fate is kind or at least tolerable to us, there might seem to be no problem in charting this course. But what if fate is cruel to us? If the road to the present has led to a good outcome, and if everything along the way is believed to have been a stage intimately linked to this outcome, then one may be prepared to validate the whole chain of events, the bad alongside the good. (For example, one might say, "Even though my marriage ended on the rocks and brought many misfortunes my way, I wouldn't have travelled the world and become the mother of these beautiful children if I hadn't married him; so if I had to do it all over again, I wouldn't change a thing." Everyone can pick his or her own similar autobiographical examples.) Nietzsche wants to push this reasoning further – perhaps quite a lot further – as when he says, "My formula for greatness in a human being is *amor fati*: that one wants nothing to be other than it is, not in the future, not in the past, not in all eternity. Not merely to endure that which happens of necessity, still less to dissemble it … but to *love* it."[41] In other words, he wants us to become beings with the courage to affirm existence rather than to live in disappointment, denial, withdrawal, and resentment, regardless of what happens. Strength and purpose evolve out of challenge and hardship, from which all of us can benefit as we move forward. Loving your fate is, for Nietzsche, the key to life. This act becomes the gold standard of self-definition and creative freedom.

In Brief …

Steven Cahn, like many other philosophers, reflects negatively on fatalism: "This is, indeed, a sorry picture of human life. We are all, according to fatalism, powerless to change our destinies. We *can* only do what we *shall* do, and what we shall do is not up to us."[42] A primary goal of the present book, however, has been to show that we both need to and are able to detach the concept of fate from fatalism and can view fate in its own right, within the rich context of lived experience. Fate has been characterized throughout this discussion as the state of things that we have no control over, that is of special significance for us, and that tasks us to respond in a self-defining way. Accordingly, we have examined multiple scenarios in which we can constructively relate to the idea and reality of fate. Some people have little or no trouble with integrating fate into their lives. Others are skeptical or hostile to the idea and to everything they think it represents. Still others are agnostic or unsure of how they feel about it all. The ultimate lesson of our inquiry is that fate is a notion we cannot ignore, which has a legitimate range of applications and enhances our perception of the world around us, and our judgment of events as they unfold, as well as of the impact they exercise upon us. This range of considerations naturally includes the milestones of birth, death, and the fortunes and misfortunes that come our way. But it also comprises many of the smaller, unpredictable, but no less important happenings that form the structures of life. And finally, fate affects us via both major and seemingly lesser world-forming events. The upshot of this investigation is that fate is one sort of anchor people rely on for building the narrative or story of their lives.

We may seek to evade fate's influence in our lives or take an attitude of disavowal or disparagement toward it. We may also embrace fate too much, for example by shifting responsibility for what we are and do onto forces or persons outside ourselves. But ultimately we can, and should, avoid such a temptation and try instead to keep things in proportion. Doing so involves developing a holistic view of ourselves and our presence in the world – one that features active, self-aware agency and self-making, but also allows a place for the things we cannot choose or change that play a role in determining our course through life. We don't have to love our fate; but we should strive to situate it within a meaningful framework of understanding that helps us move forward. What we have here is something beyond a mere acknowledgment of fate – something more like affirming oneself as best one can in the face of circumstances, and in pursuit of a worthwhile existence. This is the personal project of finding meaning that philosophers have always addressed and articulated in one fashion or another. It grows in depth with the addition of a fateful perspective on potential avenues to fulfilment, since such a perspective enables us to encompass a larger outlook on the world and on our relationships with all kinds of other people, who are our fellow travellers through life.

AFTERWORD

(I) Fate in the Time of Pandemic[1]

We can always learn more about ourselves as a species and as individuals, even if the circumstances we find ourselves in are far from ideal. It is often claimed, for example, that experiences of war or natural disasters and how we respond to them teach us important lessons. Times of adversity are points when reflecting on fate seems unavoidable, and, if we are lucky, some lasting insight is gained. Life in an era constantly haunted by the specter of COVID-19 (among other pressing major world concerns) is not a situation we would wish for ourselves or for anyone else. Perhaps we'd rather be thinking about some other, more pleasant things. But at least it can be said that thinking about fateful circumstances helps illuminate the strengths and weaknesses of the human psyche, and this can be both edifying and useful to us.

So, from the standpoint of fate, what have we learned from the COVID-19 pandemic? We seem to have gained a major awareness of how precarious our hopes, plans, and projects really are. Many have seen their dreams dashed and have lost their livelihoods or life savings. Others have become very sick and a large number across the world have died. Some have absorbed the truth that prudent behaviour may help keep us safe or prevent us from dying; but we also know a deadly disease can come our way quite unannounced and stealthily whatever precautions we may take. The outstanding message in all of this is that our life path can be altered fundamentally by a surprise revelation or a major impact of some sort at any time. But equally, such a message can help us understand that, provided our external circumstances permit, we almost always have significant scope for free choice and action that can make a substantial difference to our prospects of personal survival and wellbeing. Thus, for example, it became commonplace during the early 2020s pandemic period for people to work from home, and the lasting effect of that social change has been that many enjoy this option, or else prefer a home/office time split, and wish to keep it, which may lead to a permanent evolution in the world of employment.

Another awareness COVID-19 reinforces is that fate is as much a concept held in common as an individual one. The following example illustrates the point in a striking fashion. During the pandemic, high school students in some graduating classes experienced not only serious threats to their health and safety both inside and outside of school (like students generally), but also faced disappointing and deflating shutdowns that limited the learning opportunities, social life, extracurricular activities, and normal rites of passage for their age group. Some students, though, saw the situation as a kind of shared fate; this contributed to a unique outlook and even sparked an unusual, unexpected sense of camaraderie and optimism for these young people with respect to the future. Maybe such sanguine responses exemplify a sense that "if things can get this bad, then what comes next has to be better." Or perhaps it is just a sense that "we must be a chosen group," even if the selection process is undesirable. So, once again, we do well to avoid bland negative judgments about belief in fate as being automatically pessimistic and indicative of the avoidance of individual responsibility.

The COVID-19 pandemic appeared to produce markedly opposing responses from people. Some who are more impulsive and less thoughtful approached the situation they found themselves in with the mindset: "If I'm going to get it, I'll get it anyway no matter what

I do." Their actions during seriously risky periods of the pandemic – such as throwing parties, refusing to wear masks, and displaying witless defiance as a mark of personal freedom – manifested an attitude of not caring for their own or others' welfare. Such an attitude replicates the lazy fatalist, whom we met earlier, large as life (see pages 63–4). A more nuanced viewpoint belongs to those who have felt encouraged (if not required) by the situation at hand to reflect carefully on their own behaviour and decisions. These individuals might have argued: "I realize even the smallest mistake I make in a public place or in being slack about hygiene could give me the disease. Or I could be unfortunate and, despite my best self-defensive efforts, come into contact with a COVID-19 'superspreader' (or an asymptomatic or a presymptomatic spreader) without even knowing it. But I have to go places and do things. I have to make a living and feed my family. So I need to redouble my efforts to stay safe and hope for the best." Such a perspective allows for the very real possibility that during this dire time the outcome for oneself may be unfortunately fated. But by the same token, a more circumspect approach affirms that although there are limits to personal control, how we behave really does make a difference – perhaps all the difference – and we may save our own lives and/or the lives of others in the end. In short, if we follow the best medical advice and when necessary wear protective masks, socially distance ourselves, get tested frequently, and self-isolate when necessary then we are taking charge as much as we can. This is far better than disregarding all warnings and advice and letting circumstances decide our destiny.

Living in the present moment has its unique challenges, among which, in our era, can be counted the need to rise above the mentality of defeatism and victimization and to overcome learned helplessness. During the coronavirus pandemic, these challenges were compounded by the media. We were told over and over, for example, that "the fate of many millions of people rests on … a vaccine for COVID-19 – the only sure escape route from the pandemic."[2] Thus, we've been encouraged to think of ourselves as totally dependent on medical intervention for a healthier future, rather than as creative, assertive beings who can take charge and change the world in positive, far-reaching ways – such as by repairing our damaged relationship with the biosphere, which many scientists see as the ultimate cause of pandemics. But perhaps what is required of us is to refigure the situation we are in, seeing it as an opportunity to act, both in a self-protective way and in order to forge a forward-looking pathway. We thereby assume responsibility for our fate and seek a positive means to transcend it.

(II) The Future of Fate

Many concepts that were once potent and even dominated people's outlooks, at various times in history or in certain fields of inquiry, have now vanished from human discourse and look, retrospectively, like quaint curiosities. Some historical examples are: the divine right of kings, papal infallibility, the white man's burden, and aggressive selfishness as humans' natural condition. Examples from science are: the all-pervasive luminous ether responsible for transmitting light through empty space; phlogiston, a combustible substance allegedly residing within matter that explains fire; the geocentric or Earth-centred view of the universe (together with celestial spheres, posited to explain the apparent motion of planets and stars); skull bumps used by phrenologists to account for personality; bodily humours that supposedly explain people's dispositions and behaviours; and the vital force said to animate all living things. In an overview article titled "Tomorrow's Gods: What Is the Future of Religion?"[3] Sumit Paul-Choudhury reflects on how people's beliefs about ultimate things are changing and notes new trends that are appearing on the scene. No mention is made of fate as a competitor or a complement to faith, so it's fair to ask whether fate is on the way out, on its way to becoming a discredited, obsolete, perhaps even risible notion. Is fate itself fated to meet its own doom someday, like the concepts listed above?

The short answer is no. As we have seen, people need fate to fill in the gaps – both large and small – that they encounter in trying to make sense of existence. Fate helps us explain some things that happen to us – or at least it makes us feel we can better understand and accept them. And of course, since fate plays an intimate role within certain strands of religious belief, it will continue to do so for as long as *those* outlooks endure. We may be fairly certain, then, that fate will continue to assert itself as a source of puzzlement, challenge, and solace in the future, as it has always done. We should not, therefore, hasten to hold any memorial services for fate just yet. Perhaps instead we should heed Intisar-al-Haq's observation that "Although we do not have any rational or reasonable ground to believe in fatalism, still it will always persist in us for various reasons. It has enriched our poetry, drama and other literary or aesthetic means of expression, and it will remain as a source of consolation and inspiration for all times to come."[4] Human life is much more interesting for the presence within it of such cognitive and psychological perspectives. From this kind of observation we may further conclude that a well-rounded worldview will number fate among its essential elements.

On a practical or action-oriented level, there are additional good reasons for integrating fate into our intellectual vista. To take one pressing example, most countries have little or no evident policy to ensure food or energy security and independence for the long-term future. Without this kind of planning, however, they remain extremely vulnerable to world political events and harsh weather patterns driven by climate change. There's no magic formula for attaining beneficial long-range goals; but without them a country's fate is beyond its own control. Yet some care is required in order to avoid going too far into the domain of fatefulness. It's said that we gain pleasure and catharsis from watching tragedies unfold. And tragedies often hinge on fateful events and encounters. But while blaming fate extracts sympathy from others it can also be a form of projection and rationalization. If fate calls the shots, people needn't take responsibility for the state of the world nor even for their own lives (recall the discussion of "Doomism" in chapter 5). Another approach that concedes the impact of fate but is a little more self-assertive is the speculative or wagering perspective: "There's always the chance I might beat the odds against me and escape my destiny" (for example, by gambling or by investing in a miracle cure).

Really, however, when all is said and done, our best option is to act as if we are self-deciding, self-making beings. To choose any lesser status is to forfeit our humanity. Critics may argue that this not realistically an option because our prospects in life are determined by our DNA and other fixed factors and conditions. Or it may be said that this "choice" is simply opting to live in the mode of "as if" – a hypothetical construction of the way things are, or might be, that can easily become exposed as merely a form of wish-fulfillment. But we are probably condemned ("fated?") to lock ourselves into one vision of reality or another; and arguably the world shaped (in part at least) by the notion of free choice is a far better alternative than any other, and also one that is pragmatically more manageable.

There may still be persistent voices in our heads that demand to know whether our judgment of reality is accurate or illusory. Do we live in a multiverse where the same lives and events eternally recur, or where replica selves or Doppelgängers reside in parallel spheres of being? Could the Earth be an experimental laboratory run by a superior species, a theatre stage operated by a cosmic puppet master, or possibly even a complex computer simulation or holograph? What will happen if artificial intelligence takes over the planet and proves that we are (and always have been) merely machines? What if the world of *1984* comes to pass? These are all dire speculative hypotheses that we would have no true objective standpoint for evaluating from within, should they press in upon us. Yet some scenarios humans can control and/or prevent from occurring, while others we might just have to adapt to and learn to live with as they float in the background, leaving it to physicists, mathematicians, and cosmologists to make sense of them, as we do today. This way of resolving our questions may seem less than satisfactory. But we need to remind ourselves that life is open-ended, which means that we are never likely to reach the final story about ourselves or the universe we inhabit. For some, this existential mystery may be cause for dismay; but we can equally well interpret it as a sign that the scope of our free imagination and choice remains always beyond closure.

ACKNOWLEDGMENTS

As a fortunate person who now happily recognizes Brisbane as my home, I wish to acknowledge the Jagera and Turrbal peoples, the Traditional Custodians of the lands and waters of Meanjin, which is where this book was written and what this place was once called. I also take this opportunity to pay my respects to Elders past, present, and emerging and to affirm the ongoing contributions of First Peoples to Australian and world culture.

Fate has enabled me to finish writing this book and to find a publisher for it. For those things, I am very grateful. The greatest thanks, as always, goes to my wonderful wife and partner, Louise Noble, for her love, support, encouragement, ideas, advice, editing, discussions, and for reading my entire manuscript and helping with technical problems. (I also owe the choice of title and publisher to her.) Thanks to my children Jason, Tim, and Zoé for their positive outlooks on my work-in-progress. Thanks to Rob Banks for his input at the early phase of conceptualizing this project and for his enthusiasm and suggestions. Thanks to Steph and Bryan McLennan for safekeeping an electronic copy and updates of my manuscript at separate premises from mine during various stages of its development.

I appreciate the use of the Queensland State Library, Brisbane City Council Main Library, University of Queensland Library, and the online resources of libraries at the University of New England (Australia) and Queen's University (Canada). I am indebted as well to the University of New England, Armidale, NSW, Australia, for my ongoing appointment as adjunct professor, attached to the School of Humanities, Arts and Social Sciences.

Finally, I want to express my deep appreciation to my two anonymous manuscript referees and my commissioning editor, Khadija Coxon, for their important critical contributions, which made this a better book and helped it reach publication. In addition, Kathryn Simpson's thoughtful and sensitive copyediting has been invaluable. My thanks to her for her overall interest and careful attention to detail. I do not know the names of everyone responsible for the book's splendid cover design, and for other editorial, marketing, promotion, and miscellaneous processes, but I warmly appreciate all your efforts on my behalf.

NOTES

PREFACE

1 This expression is borrowed from Albert Camus, "Entre Oui et Non," in *L'envers et l'endroit* (1937); trans. as "Betwixt and Between" or "The Right Side and the Wrong Side"; pub. as "Between Yes and No," *World Review*, new series (13 March 1950): 39.

CHAPTER ONE

1 Seneca, *Oedipus*, trans. James F. Pfundstein, i, 993–4. *Seneca's Oedipus: A Translation in Alliterative Verse*, https://jamesenge.com/Seneca-Oedipus.JMP.trans.pdf.

2 David Malouf, *The Conversations at Curlow Creek* (London: Vintage, 1997), 168.

3 Charles Foster, *Being a Human: Adventures in 40,000 Years of Consciousness* (London: Profile, 2021), 100.

4 *Que Será, Será (Whatever Will Be, Will Be)*, written by Jay Livingston and Ray Evans, sung by Doris Day.

5 William Shakespeare, *As You Like It* (1599), act ii, scene vii, 139–40.

6 Denis Diderot (1713–1784), the famous Enlightenment encyclopedist, for example, plays with this theme in his eighteenth-century experimental novel *Jacques the Fatalist and His Master* (written 1765–80; first pub. 1796), trans. Michael Henry (London: Penguin Books, 1986).

7 Lisa Halliday, *Asymmetry* (London: Granta, 2018), 188.

8 Marguerite Young, quoted by Roy Newquist, *Conversations* (New York: Rand McNally, 1967).

9 Steven Carroll, *Spirit of Progress* (Sydney: Fourth Estate, 2015), 94.

10 Ibid., 290, 293, 300.

11 Arthur Schopenhauer, *Counsels and Maxims*, in *The Essays of Arthur Schopenhauer*, trans. T. Bailey Saunders, ch. 4, sec. 52 (emphasis in

original). Project Gutenberg EBooks: http://www.gutenberg.org/files/10715/10715-h/10715-h.htm#link2H_4_0054.

12 Henry David Thoreau, Journal 6, ch. 5 (27 April 1854), 226. https://www.walden.org/wp-content/uploads/2016/02/Journal-6-Chapter-5.pdf.

13 William James, *Habit* (New York: Henry Holt, 1914), 67.

14 Henry Miller, *Big Sur and the Oranges of Hieronymous Bosch* (New York: New Directions, 1957), 325.

15 Marjan Kamali, *The Stationery Shop* (New York: Gallery Books, 2019), 4.

16 Rituparnaa, "Superstitions across Different Countries – An Overview," Dazeinfo, 22 June 2010, https://dazeinfo.com/2010/06/22/superstitions-across-different-countries-an-overview.

17 Åke V. Ström, "Scandinavian Belief in Fate: A Comparison between Pre-Christian and Post-Christian Times," in *Fatalistic Beliefs in Religion, Folklore, and Literature* (papers read at the Symposium on Fatalistic Beliefs held at Åbo on the 7–9 of September, 1964), ed. Helmer Ringgren (Stockholm: Almqvist & Wiksell, 1967), 86.

18 Earl Conee, "Fatalism," in Ted Sider and Earl Conee, *Riddles of Existence: A Guided Tour of Existence*, new edition (Oxford: Oxford University Press, 2014), 26.

19 Blaise Pascal, *Pensées* (1670), rev. edition, trans. A.J. Krailsheimer (Harmondsworth, UK: Penguin Books, 1973). See, for example, sec. 199.

20 Helmer Ringgren, "The Problem of Fatalism," in *Fatalistic Beliefs in Religion, Folklore, and Literature*, ed. Ringgren, 8.

21 Shiryn Ghermezian, "Jewish Tennis Star Diego Schwartzman Highlights Lessons from Family's Holocaust History," *Algemeiner*, 30 January 2020, https://www.algemeiner.com/2020/01/30/jewish-tennis-star-diego-schwartzman-highlights-lessons-from-familys-holocaust-history-in-new-essay.

22 Jérôme Ferrari, *The Sermon on the Fall of Rome*, trans. Geoffrey Strachan (London: MacLehose Press, 2014), 44, 84.

23 Gelven, *Why Me?*, 156.

24 Niall Williams, *This Is Happiness* (London: Bloomsbury, 2020), 346 (emphasis in original).

25 Isabel Allende, *Violeta*, trans. Frances Riddle (London: Bloomsbury Publishing, 2022), 252.

26 Psalm 33:6; Genesis 1:3 (King James trans.).

27 Rice, "Fatalism."

28 Taylor, *Metaphysics*, 55.

29 Cambridge online dictionary; https://dictionary.cambridge.orgdictionary/english/fatalism.

30 Charles Gounod, *Faust* (1859); Christopher Marlowe, *The Tragical History of Doctor Faustus* (c. 1587); Johann von Goethe, *Faust* (part i, 1808, part ii, 1832); Thomas Mann, *Doctor Faustus* (1947).

31 Marie Jones, for example, argues that even though there are many ways in which we can choose to realize our destiny, it is ultimately a fated outcome that we cannot avoid. See Marie Jones, *Destiny vs Choice: The Scientific and Spiritual Evidence behind Fate and Free Will* (Pompton Plains, NJ: The Career Press, 2011), 17.

32 Fiori Giovanni, *Defy Your Destiny: Make Your Most Painful Walk Your Most Triumphant Journey* (Melbourne: SAGT, 2019).

33 S.G. Browne, *Fated* (London: Piatkus, 2011).

34 Dashiell Hammett, *The Maltese Falcon* (New York: Vintage Crime/ Black Lizard, 1992), 64. (Originally pub. 1930.)

35 Taylor, *Metaphysics*, 54.

36 Graham Lawton, "Where Are Your Boundaries?" *New Scientist* (12 December 2020): 37–8.

37 Clare Wilson, "How Likely Are You?" *New Scientist* (12 December 2020): 34.

38 Julian F. Woods, "Fatalism, Indian," in *Routledge Encyclopedia of Philosophy*, ed. Edward Craig, (London: Routledge, 1998), vol. 3, 566.

39 Joanna Gillan, "The Aztec Calendar Wheel and the Philosophy of Time," *Ancient Origins*, 28 March 2019, https://www.ancient-origins.net/news/aztec-calendar-wheel-and-philosophy-time-001345.

40 William Shakespeare, *Henry V* (1599), act iii, scene vi.

41 Whalen Lai, "Fatalism in Chinese Philosophy, in *Encyclopedia of Asian Philosophy*, ed. Oliver Leaman (London and New York: Routledge, 2001), 196 (emphasis added).

42 Diogenes Laërtius (180–240 CE), "Zeno," in *Lives of the Eminent Philosophers* (third century CE), trans. R.D. Hicks, vol. ii, bk vii, ch. 1, Loeb Classical Library (Cambridge, MA: Harvard University Press, 1925), secs 149, 254. http://penelope.uchicago.edu.

43 Cicero, *On Divination* (44 BCE), 1, 125–6, in *The Hellenistic Philosophers: Volume I – Translation of the Principal Sources with Philosophical Commentary*, ed. and trans. A.A. Long and D.N. Sedley, (Cambridge, UK: Cambridge University Press, 1987), "Stoic Physics," sec. 55 ("Causation and Fate"), 337.

44 For example, by Critchlow, *The Science of Fate.*

45 Bolle, "Fate," 2998.

46 That explains why belief in omens and deities is so hard to refute: if faith in them proves to be wrong, we must have misread the signs or else the truth is beyond our understanding.

47 This view is sometimes called "superdeterminism"; see Michael Brooks, "Is Everything Predetermined?" *New Scientist* (15 May 2021): 36–40.

48 Edward Craig, "Fatalism," in *Routledge Encyclopedia of Philosophy*, ed. Craig, vol. 3, 564.

49 Those who are interested in pursuing this issue might have a look at the following: Jordan Howard Sobel, *Puzzles for the Will* (Toronto: University of Toronto Press, 1998); Leonard W. Doob, *Inevitability: Determinism, Fatalism, and Destiny* (New York: Greenwood Press, 1988).

50 See, for example, Jim Al-Khalili, *The World According to Physics* (Princeton: Princeton University Press, 2020), 155–62.

51 James Woodward and Lauren Ross, "Scientific Explanation," *Stanford Encyclopedia of Philosophy* (summer 2021 edition), ed. Edward N. Zalta, https://plato.stanford.edu/archives/sum2021/entries/scientific-explanation; G. Randolph Mayes, "Theories of Explanation," *Internet Encyclopedia of Philosophy*, ed. James Fieser and Bradley Dowden, https://iep.utm.edu/explanat.

52 See, for example, Matteo Colombo, "Experimental Philosophy of Explanation Rising: The Case for a Plurality of Concepts of *Explanation*," *Cognitive Science* 41 (2017): 503–17, onlinelibrary.wiley.com/doi/pdf/10.1111/cogs.12340; Andrew Brenner et al., "Metaphysical Explanation," *Stanford Encyclopedia of Philosophy*, ed. Edward N. Zalta (Winter 2021 edition), https://plato.stanford.edu/archives/win2021/entries/metaphysical-explanation.

53 Kareem Khalifa, *Understanding, Explanation, and Scientific Knowledge* (Cambridge: Cambridge University Press, 2017).

54 Gelven, *Why Me?*, 7.

55 Jane Smiley, *A Thousand Acres* (New York: Anchor Books, 2003), 22.

56 Rachel Cusk, *The Bradshaw Variations* (London: Faber and Faber, 2009), 221.

57 Joanne Harris, "Come in, Mr Lowry, Your Number Is Up!," in *Jigs & Reels* (London: Doubleday, 2004), 189.

CHAPTER TWO

1 Sumerian proverb, Collection 2 + 6: c.6.1.02 at the Electronic Text Corpus of Sumerian Literature (2016 update), etcsl.orinst.ox.ac.uk/#. Earliest known written literature, third millennium BCE.

2 Neil Oliver, *The Story of the World in 100 Moments* (London: Bantam Press, 2021), 146.

3 Haitham Rashid, Sunni Lebanese, on the prospect of imminent war between Israel and Hezbollah, as quoted in Martin Chulov, "Hezbollah's Long War Comes out of the Shadows," *Guardian Weekly*, 14 April 2023: 12.

4 Gabriele Ruiu, "Is Fatalism a Cultural Belief?: An Empirical Analysis on the Origin of Fatalistic Tendencies," MRPA Paper 41705, University Library of Munich, 16 July 2012, 4 (emphasis in original), https://ideas.repec.org/p/pra/mprapa/41705.html.

5 Oliver, *The Story of the World*, 28.

6 Carly Minsky, "Physicists Are Studying Mysterious 'Bubbles of Nothing' That Eat Spacetime," 5 March 2020, www.vice.com.

7 Bolle, "Fate," 2998.

8 Stephen Herbert Langdon, "Semitic Mythology," in *The Mythology of All Races*, ed. John Arnott MacCulloch (New York: Cooper Square Publishers, 1964), vol. 5, 24, 398 n. 101.

9 J. Bruce Long, "Webs and Nets," in *Encyclopedia of Religion*, second edition, ed. Lindsay Jones (Detroit: Macmillan Reference USA/Thomson Gale, 2005), vol. 14, 9713.

10 Giulia Piccaluga, "Knots," trans. Roger DeGaris, in *Encyclopedia of Religion*, ed. Jones, vol. 8, 341.

11 According to the *Oxford English Dictionary*, "the expression 'spin a thread' [was] used as far back as the 1300s in the sense of 'tell a tale.'" It is commonly noted that "spin a yarn" derives from nineteenth-century sailors' and fishermen's practice of telling tales while tending to yarn supplies during idle moments at sea. See Patricia T. O'Conner and Stewart Kellerman, "Spinning a Yarn," *Grammarphobia*, 21 October 2015, https://www.grammarphobia.com/blog/2015/10/yarn.html. In Australian usage (dating from the 1840s), a "yarning circle" is "a gathering of people who sit in a circle to share experience, knowledge, or ideas; a place where such a meeting is held." This meaning is recognized among both Indigenous and non-Indigenous populations. See Australian National University, School of Literature, Languages and Linguistics, "Yarning Circle," https://slll.cass.anu.edu.au/centres/andc/yarning-circle.

12 Bolle, "Fate," 3001.

13 Visser, *Beyond Fate*, 118.

14 Jakob Anil Ottesen Larsen and P.J. Rhodes, "Fate," in *The Oxford Classical Dictionary*, 4th ed., ed. Simon Hornblower et al. (Oxford: Oxford University Press, 2012), 569.

15 Julian Baggini, *How the World Thinks: A Global History of Philosophy* (London: Granta, 2018), 203.

16 Ronald Grambo, "Problems of Fatalism: A Blueprint for Further Research," *Folklore* 99, no. 1 (1988): 12.

17 William B. Irvine, *A Guide to the Good Life: The Ancient Art of Stoic Joy* (Oxford: Oxford University Press, 2009), 102.

18 John Sellars, *Lessons in Stoicism: What Ancient Philosophers Teach Us about How to Live* (London: Penguin Books, 2020), 43 (emphases in original).

19 Kai Whiting and Leonidas Konstantakos, *Being Better: Stoicism for a World Worth Living In* (Novato, CA: New World Library, 2021), 58.

20 Helmer Ringgren, ed. *Fatalistic Beliefs in Religion, Folklore, and Literature* (papers read at the Symposium on Fatalistic Beliefs held at Åbo on the 7–9 of September, 1964) (Stockholm: Almqvist & Wiksell, 1967).

21 Bolle, "Fate," 3005.

22 Uno Holmberg, "Finno-Ugric, Siberian Mythology," in *The Mythology of All Races*, ed. MacCulloch, vol. 4, 394–5.

23 W. Max Müller, "Egyptian Mythology," in *The Mythology of All Races*, ed. Louis Herbert Gray (New York: Cooper Square Publishers, 1964), vol. 12, 35–6, 39.

24 Anita Sujoldžić, "Vlachs," in *Encyclopedia of World Cultures*, ed. Linda A. Bennett (New York: G.K. Hall/London: Prentice Hall International, 1994), vol. 4, 275.

25 Ronald Johnson, "Persians," in *Encyclopedia of World Cultures*, ed. John Middleton (Boston: G.K. Hall, 1995), vol. 9, 280.

26 Abd-al-Hosayn Zarrinkub, "Fatalism," in *Encyclopaedia Iranica*, ed. Ehsan Yarshater (24 January 2012), iranicaonline.org/articles/fatalism.

27 Robert Tonkinson and Ronald M. Berndt, "Australian Aboriginal Peoples," in *Encyclopaedia Britannica* (2019), https://www.britannica.com/topic/Australian-Aboriginal.

28 Hartley Burr Alexander, "North American Mythology," in *The Mythology of All Races*, Gray, ed., vol. 10, 82.

29 Alice C. Fletcher and Francis La Flesche, *The Omaha Tribe* (1911) (New York: Johnson Reprint Corporation, 1970), 598, 599.

30 Brian Fallon, *Tony O'Malley: Painter in Exile* (Dublin: Arts Council; Belfast: Arts Council of Northern Ireland, 1984), 25.

31 The usual source for this information is the composer's biography written by his wife: Alma Mahler, *Gustav Mahler: Memories and Letters*, third edition, ed. Donald Mitchell; trans. Basil Creighton, (London: John Murray, 1973), 70.

32 Peter Frankopan, *The Silk Roads: A New History of the World* (London: Bloomsbury, 2016), 272.

33 Mary Costello, *The River Capture* (Melbourne: Text Publishing, 2019), 223.

34 Grambo, "Problems of Fatalism," 26.

35 Visser, *Beyond Fate*, 91.

36 Adolf Grünbaum, "Free Will and Laws of Human Behavior," *American Philosophical Quarterly* 8 (1971): 302.

CHAPTER THREE

1 Lady Mary Wortley Montague (also known as Mary Pierrepont, 1689–1762), in *The Letters of Lady Mary Wortley Montague*, ed. Sarah Josepha Buell Hale, rev. ed. (Boston: Roberts Brothers, 1876), 151. Letter written in 1759.

2 Roy Jacobsen, *The Unseen*, trans. Don Bartlett and Don Shaw (London: MacLehose Press, 2016), 69. This is a piece of Norwegian fishermen's folk wisdom.

3 Daphne du Maurier, *The Scapegoat* (London: Virago Press, 2004), 21, 30.

4 Anthony Doerr, *About Grace* (New York: Penguin Books, 2005), 388.

5 Jonathan Schell, *The Fate of the Earth* (New York: Alfred A. Knopf, 1982).

6 Jonathan Freedland, "Fate Could Have Put Any of Us in Those Migrant Boats," *Guardian Weekly*, 17 March 2023, 46.

7 *Kismet*, musical adapted by Charles Lederer and Luther Davis from a 1911 play by Edward Knoblock, with lyrics and music by Robert Wright and George Forrest. Most of the music was adapted from Russian composer Alexander Borodin (1833–1887). See "Kismet," *Wikipedia*, https://en.wikipedia.org/wiki/Kismet.

8 Catherine Zuckerman, "Newfound Tiny Planet May Be a Glimpse of Earth's Ultimate Fate," *National Geographic*, 4 April 2019, https://www.nationalgeographic.com/science/2019/04/planet-found-orbiting-white-dwarf-may-be-a-glimpse-of-earths-fate.

9 Matthew Knott, "Fall Guy," *Sydney Morning Herald Good Weekend*, 24 October 2020, 10.

10 Sebastian Faulks, *Paris Echo* (London: Hutchinson, 2018), 160.

11 Oliver Burkeman, "Future Imperfect," *Guardian Weekly*, 18 January 2019, 43.

12 Simon Cleary, *The Comfort of Figs* (St Lucia, Queensland, Australia: University of Queensland Press, 2009), 147.

13 Ibid., 176.

14 Thomas à Kempis (1380–1471), *The Imitation of Christ* (first published c. 1400), trans. Aloysius Croft and Harold Bolton (Milwaukee: Bruce Publishing, 1940), bk. 1, ch. 19, https://web.archive.org/web/20040711045414/http://www.ccel.org/ccel/kempis/imitation.all.html#ONE.

15 Steven Millhauser, *We Others: New and Selected Stories* (New York: Alfred A. Knopf, 2011), 164.

16 Bradford Morrow, *The Forgers* (New York: The Mysterious Press, 2014), 221.

17 Amos Oz, *A Tale of Love and Darkness*, trans. Nicholas de Lange (Orlando: Harcourt, 2004), 39.

18 Arthur Schopenhauer, *Counsels and Maxims* (1851), in *The Essays of Arthur Schopenhauer*, trans. T. Bailey Saunders, chap. 4, sec. 51. Project Gutenberg EBooks, http://www.gutenberg.org/files/10715/10715-h/10715-h.htm#link2H_4_0054.

19 Horace, *Odes* (first appeared 23 BCE), bk 1, no. 9, 1.13. See Horace, *The Complete Odes and Epodes*, trans. W.G. Shepherd (Harmondsworth, Middlesex: Penguin Books, 1983), bk 1, no. 9, 78.

20 Corinne DeRuiter, "Fate Map" (last modified 3 July 2018), *Embryo Project Encyclopedia*, https://embryo.asu.edu/pages/fate-map.

21 Alice Wexler, *Mapping Fate: A Memoir of Family, Risk, and Genetic Research* (Berkeley: University of California Press, 1996). A life story with a similar perspective has recently appeared in print: *Fighting Fate* by Justin Yerbury (Melbourne: Affirm Press, 2023), which details the author's struggle with motor neurone disease.

22 Ibid., 273.

CHAPTER FOUR

1 Andrea Iacona, "Future Contingents." In *Internet Encyclopedia of Philosophy*, ed. James Fieser and Bradley Dowden, https://www.iep.utm.edu/fut-cont.

2 Stephen Hawking, *Black Holes and Baby Universes and Other Essays* (1993), 133–5, https://www.lifehack.org/articles/communication/20-inspirational-quotes-stephen-hawking-everyone-should-read.html.

3 Eilstein, *Life Contemplative, Life Practical*, 34 (emphasis in original).

4 Anthony Doerr, *About Grace* (New York: Penguin Books, 2005), 247.

5 Bernstein, *Fatalism*, 8.

6 Aristotle, *On Interpretation* (written in 350 BCE), sec. 1, ch\. 9. See trans. by E.M. Edghill, Internet Classics Archive, 1994, http://classics.mit.edu/Aristotle/interpretation.mb.txt.

7 Eilstein, *Life Contemplative, Life Practical*, 87.

8 Edward Craig, "Fatalism," in *Routledge Encyclopedia of Philosophy*, ed. Edward Craig (London and New York: Routledge, 1998), vol. 3, 564.

9 It's interesting how often we disregard this insight, referring as we do to "the foreseeable future" and making firm assertions about a day, a year, or some indefinite period into the future. But then again, given the kind of beings we are, we have to plan our lives beyond the present, or live mentally in the future to some extent. Or (if fatalism is true) we at least need to pretend to do so.

10 See note 6 above.

11 Jan Łukasiewicz, "On Determinism," (1922), trans. Z. Jordan, in *Polish Logic, 1920–1939*, ed. Storrs McCall (Oxford: Clarendon Press, 1967), 19–39, http://sshieh.web.wesleyan.edu/wescourses/2013f/231/e-texts/Lukasiewicz,%20On%20Determinism.pdf.

12 Richard Taylor, "Fatalism," *Philosophical Review* 71 (1962): 56.

13 Ibid., 58. An entire, very challenging volume of essays has been devoted to attacking Taylor's early fatalistic argument: see Wallace, *Fate, Time, and Language.*

14 Taylor, *Metaphysics*, 63–6.

15 Ibid., 58–63.

16 Sophocles, *Oedipus Rex* (first performed 430–426 BCE).

17 W. Somerset Maugham, "Sheppy," in *The Collected Plays of W. Somerset Maugham* (London: William Heinemann, 1931), 299. "Appointment in Samarra" has also been used by American author John O'Hara as the title of a novel, and reappears in 2017 in the opening episode of the *Sherlock Holmes* TV series starring Benedict Cumberbatch. A number of additional fatalistic tales are summarized by Eilstein in *Life Contemplative, Life Practical*, 39–43.

18 Abd-al-Hosayn Zarrinkub, "Fatalism," in *Encyclopaedia Iranica*, ed. Ehsan Yarshater (24 January 2012). iranicaonline.org/articles/fatalism. The *Qur'an* is believed to be the words of Allah, while the *Hadith* is said to report the words of Muhammad, his family, and his followers.

19 Matthew 6:10; Luke 22:42.

20 John 6:38; Acts 21:14.

21 Notice, however, that God, in this scenario, also has the power to violate the principle of logic concerning truth and falsity that Aristotle, Taylor, and many others hold to be sacrosanct.

22 Interestingly, philosophers in recent decades have proposed a secular theory similar in nature to that which features all moments in time being simultaneously open to God. According to the complex "block universe" view (also known as "eternalism"), the relativity theory of Albert Einstein (1879–1955) entails that time does not actually "flow" in the past-present-future pattern we are accustomed to. All parameters of time coexist, and therefore the future is already as real as past and present. The fatalistic overtones of this position speak for themselves. See Dan Falk, "A Debate over the Physics of Time," *Quanta Magazine* (19 July 2016), https://www.quantamagazine.org/a-debate-over-the-physics-of-time-20160719.

CHAPTER FIVE

1 Adolf Hitler, *Mein Kampf*, trans. Ralph Manheim (Boston: Houghton Mifflin, 1943), 296.

2 Adolf Hitler, *Speech on the 19th Anniversary of the "Beer Hall Putsch"* (8 November 1942), https://www.jewishvirtuallibrary.org/adolf-hitler-speech-on-the-19th-anniversary-of-the-ldquo-beer-hall-putsch-rdquo-november-1942.

3 Jean-Paul Sartre, *Being and Nothingness: An Essay on Phenomenological Ontology* (first pub. 1943), trans. Hazel E. Barnes (New York: Philosophical Library, 1956), 59.

4 Valerie M. Hudson, Bonnie Ballif-Spanvill, Mary Caprioli, and Chad F. Emmett, *Sex and World Peace* (New York: Columbia University Press, 2012).

5 See, for example, Anne Karpf, "We All Benefit from a More Gender-Equal Society. Even Men," *Guardian*, 8 March 2020, https://www.theguardian.com/commentisfree/2020/mar/08/gender-equal-international-womens-day-men; Government of Victoria (Australia), "The Benefits of Gender Equality," 30 March 2021, http://www.vic.gov.au/benefits-gender-equality; Canadian Women's Foundation, "5 Ways Gender Equality Benefits Everyone," 2 February 2022, https://canadianwomen.org/blog/5-ways-gender-equality-benefits-everyone.

6 "Nations with Anti-LGBT Laws: 49% Muslim, 44% Christian," updated April 2022, *Erasing 76 Crimes News Site*, https://76crimes.com/nations-with-anti-lgbt-laws-49-muslim-44-christian/?gclid=EAIaIQobChMIn7LjnpS6_gIVSFtgCh1XOQqrEAAYAiAAEgJLnfD_BwE.

7 Patience Atuhaire, "Uganda Anti-Homosexuality Bill: Life in Prison for Saying You're Gay," *BBC News*, 22 March 2023, https://www.bbc.com/news/world-africa-65034343.

8 *World Book Encyclopedia* (Chicago: World Book, 2019), vol. 16, 62.

9 Russell McGregor, "The Doomed Race: A Scientific Axiom of the Late Nineteenth Century," *Australian Journal of Politics and History* 39 (2008): 14.

10 See Angela Saini, *Superior: The Return of Race Science* (Boston: Beacon Press, 2019).

11 Saurabh Dube, "Untouchables, Religions of," in *Encyclopedia of Religion*, ed. Lindsay Jones, 2nd ed. (Detroit: Macmillan Reference USA/ Thomson Gale, 2005), vol. 14, 9474.

12 Ibid., 9476.

13 Rita Jalali, "Caste and Inherited Status," in *Encyclopedia of Sociology* (2001), https://www.encyclopedia.com/social-sciences/encyclopedias-almanacs-transcripts-and-maps/caste-and-inherited-status.

14 Australian Government, Australian Law Reform Commission, "02. Genetics and Human Health: A Primer, Genetic Difference: Genotype and Phenotype" (last modified 22 June 2018), https://www.alrc.gov.au/publications/2-genetics-and-human-health-primer/genetic-difference-genotype-and-phenotype.

15 Robert Plomin, *Blueprint: How DNA Makes Us Who We Are* (London: Allen Lane, 2018), 5. According to Stanley Fields and Mark Johnston, *Genetic Twists of Fate* (Cambridge, MA: MIT Press, 2010), 208, our appearance and internal biological processes are unique to us, owing to the fact that "a small fraction, about 0.1 per cent, of each individual's DNA code is slightly different from everyone else's."

16 Ibid., 31.

17 Ibid., 163.

18 Garland E. Allen, "Eugenics," in *Encyclopedia of Life Sciences*, publishing director Gina Fullerlove, (London: Nature Publishing Group, 2002), vol. 6, 568. Allen is quoting from A. Myerson et al., *Eugenical Sterilization: A Reorientation of the Problem* (New York: Macmillan, 1936).

19 Alexandra Minna Stern, "Forced Sterilization Policies in the US Targeted Minorities and Those with Disabilities – And Lasted into the 21st Century," 23 September 2020, Michigan Institute for Healthcare Policy and Innovation, University of Michigan, https://ihpi.umich.edu/news/forced-sterilization-policies-us-targeted-minorities-and-those-disabilities-and-lasted-21st#:~:text=Iowa%20and%20Michigan.-,Eugenics,and%20genetics%20to%20human%20breeding.

20 Allen, "Eugenics," 571; Edwin Black, "Hitler's Debt to America," *Guardian*, 6 February 2004, theguardian.com/uk/2004/feb/06/race.usa.

21 "Who Were the Victims?" *Holocaust Encyclopedia*, United States Holocaust Memorial Museum, 4 March 2020, encyclopedia.ushmm.org/content/en/article/mosaic-of-victims-an-overview.

22 Sui-Lee Wee, "China Uses DNA to Track Its People, with the Help of American Expertise," *New York Times*, 21 February 2019, https://www.nytimes.com/2019/02/21/business/china-xinjiang-uighur-dna-thermo-fisher.html. See also Peter Frankopan, *The New Silk Roads: The Present and Future of the World* (London: Bloomsbury, rev./updated ed., 2019), 103–6; "Torment of the Uyghurs," *Economist*, 17–23 October 2020, 9–10.

23 International Consortium of Investigative Journalists, "The China Cables," 24 November 2019, icij.org/investigations/china-cables/.

24 ABC News (Australia), "China Imposes Forced Abortion, Sterilization on Uyghurs, Investigation Shows," 30 June 2020, https://www.abc.net.au/news/2020-06-30/china-forces-birth-control-on-uyghurs-to-suppress-population/12404912; Gulbahar Haitiwaji with Rozenn Margat, "How I

Survived a Chinese 'Re-Education' Camp for Uighurs," trans. Edward Gauvin, *Guardian Weekly*, 22 January 2021, 40–4; Matthew Hill, David Campanale, and Joel Gunter, "'Their Goal Is to Destroy Everyone': Uighur Camp Detainees Allege Systematic Rape," BBC *News*, 2 February 2021, bbc.com/news/world-asia-china-55794071.

25 See Tahir Hamut Izgil, *Waiting to be Arrested at Night: A Uyghur Poet's Memoir of China's Genocide*, trans. Joshua L. Freeman (New York: Penguin Press, 2023).

26 For example, Genesis 12:1–3; Deuteronomy 1:8, 7:6, 14:2.

27 See C.T. McIntire, "Free Will and Predestination: Christian Concepts," in *Encyclopedia of Religion*, ed. Jones, vol. 5, 3206–9.

28 A.G. Palladino, "Predestination (in Catholic Theology)," in *New Catholic Encyclopedia*, ed. Berard L. Marthaler, second edition (Detroit: Thomson Gale in association with the Catholic University of America, 2002), vol. 11, 647–53.

29 See, for example, *Freedom, Fatalism, and Foreknowledge*, ed. Fischer and Todd.

30 Brian G. Armstrong, "Calvin, John," in *Encyclopedia of Religion*, ed. Jones, vol. 3, 32.

31 John Calvin, *Institutes of the Christian Religion* (first published 1536), 3.21.5; quoted by R. Matzerath and P. Soergel in "Calvinism," *New Catholic Encyclopedia*, ed. Marthaler, vol. 2, 893.

32 W. Montgomery Watt and Asma Afsaruddin, "Free Will and Predestination: Islamic Concepts," in *Encyclopedia of Religion*, ed. Jones, vol. 5, 3209.

33 Qur'ān 9:51; 56:60.

34 Ibid., 18:23–4. https://quran.com/en/al-kahf/23-24.

35 Julian Baggini, *How the World Thinks: A Global History of Philosophy* (London: Granta, 2018), 329.

36 Helmer Ringgren, "Islamic Fatalism," in *Fatalistic Beliefs in Religion, Folklore, and Literature*, ed. Helmer Ringgren (papers read at the Symposium on Fatalistic Beliefs held at Åbo on the 7–9 of September, 1964) (Stockholm: Almqvist & Wiksell, 1967), 59.

37 Watt and Afsaruddin, "Free Will and Predestination: Islamic Concepts," 3210.

38 See "Fate of the Unlearned," *Wikipedia*, https://en.wikipedia.org/wiki/Fate_of_the_unlearned.

39 Jennifer Huizen, "What to Know about Eco-Anxiety," *Medical News Today*, 19 December 2019, https://www.medicalnewstoday.com/articles/327354.

40 Callum Roberts, *The Ocean of Life: The Fate of Man and the Sea* (New York: Viking Penguin, 2012); Sylvia A. Earle, *The World Is Blue: How Our*

Fate and the Ocean's Are One (Washington, DC: National Geographic Society, 2009).

41 Amanda Little, *The Fate of Food: What We'll Eat in a Bigger, Hotter, Smarter World* (New York: Harmony, 2019).

42 Wes Jackson and Robert Jensen, *An Inconvenient Apocalypse: Environmental Collapse, Climate Crisis, and the Fate of Humanity* (Notre Dame, IN: University of Notre Dame Press, 2022).

43 Richard Flanagan, "Enjoying the Company of Birds Is to Know Inconsolable Sadness," *Guardian Weekly*, 8 November 2019, 28.

44 Dagomar Degroot, "Little Ice Age Lessons: Towards a New Climate History," www.historicalclimatology.com, 22 March 2021; Dagomar Degroot et al., "Towards a Rigorous Understanding of Societal Responses to Climate Change," *Nature* 591 (25 March 2021): 539–50.

45 Laurie Leybourn, "Worsening Climate Shocks Risk Distracting from Efforts to Reduce Carbon Emissions, Creating 'Doom Loop,' Report Warns," 16 February 2023, https://ipp.org.

46 Tim Winton, "Complacency and Fatalism Are a Ticket to Hell in a Handcart," *Guardian Weekly* (26 April 2019): 28.

47 Hannah Devlin, "Road to a Cure: A Vaccine Is Our Only Hope. What Are the Chances for Its Success?" *Guardian Weekly*, 1 May 2020, 18.

48 Vasily Grossman, *Life and Fate*, trans. Robert Chandler (New York: New York Review of Books, 2006). Publisher's description, Amazon.com.

49 Martin Meredith, *The Fate of Africa: A History of the Continent Since Independence*, revised and updated edition (New York: Public Affairs, 2011).

50 Michael F. Holt, *The Fate of Their Country: Politicians, Slavery Extension, and the Coming of the Civil War* (New York: Hill and Wang, 2004). Publisher's description, Amazon.com.

51 John Gray, *Gray's Anatomy* (London: Allen Lane, 2009), 298–9.

52 John Scott, "Progress," in *Oxford Dictionary of Sociology*, ed. John Scott and Gordon Marshall, 4th ed. (Oxford: Oxford University Press, 2019), https://www.oxfordreference.com.ezproxy.slq.qld.gov.au/view/10.1093/acref//9780199683581.001.0001/acref-9780199683581-e-1818.

53 George Washington, General Orders, 2 July 1776, in *The Writings of George Washington, from the Original Manuscript Sources, 1745–1799*, ed. John C. Fitzpatrick (Washington, DC: US Government Printing Office, 1931–44), vol. 5 (1932), 211.

54 Henry Wadsworth Longfellow, "The Landlord's Tale: Paul Revere's Ride," in *Tales of a Wayside Inn* (Boston: Ticknor and Fields, 1864), 22.

55 Bruce Pascoe, *Dark Emu: Aboriginal Australia and the Birth of Agriculture*, new edition (Broome, Western Australia: Magabala Books, 2018), 3.

56 Charles de Gaulle, speech at the University of Strasbourg, 22 November 1959, cited in Éric Anceau, "De Gaulle and Europe," *EHNE: Digital Encyclopedia of European History*, https://ehne.fr/en/encyclopedia/themes/political-europe/arbiters-and-arbitration-in-europe-beginning-modern-times/de-gaulle-and-europe.
57 Bolle, "Fate," 2998–9.
58 Sebastian Barry, *The Temporary Gentleman* (London: Faber and Faber, 2014), 86.

CHAPTER SIX

1 Heraclitus, *On the Universe*, fragment 121, trans. W.H.S. Jones, in *Hippocrates*, vol. 4, trans. W.H.S. Jones et al., Loeb Classical Library no. 150 (London: Heineman, 2010).
2 William Shakespeare, *The Rape of Lucrece* (1594), line 1069.
3 Anonymous. Posted in public places, and otherwise quoted, in many countries.
4 Helmer Ringgren, "The Problem of Fatalism," in *Fatalistic Beliefs in Religion, Folklore, and Literature*, ed. Helmer Ringgren (papers read at the Symposium on Fatalistic Beliefs held at Åbo on the 7–9 of September 1964) (Stockholm: Almqvist & Wiksell, 1967), 7.
5 Gelven, *Why Me?*, 8 (emphasis in original).
6 Amor Towles, *A Gentleman in Moscow* (London: Windmill, 2017), 80.
7 Heather Rose, *The Museum of Modern Love* (Sydney: Allen & Unwin, 2018), 72.
8 Eilstein, *Life Contemplative, Life Practical*, 10 (emphasis in original).
9 Mogens Brøndsted, "The Transformations of the Concept of Fate in Literature," in *Fatalistic Beliefs in Religion, Folklore, and Literature*, ed. Ringgren, 172.
10 G. Faggin, "Fate and Fatalism, in *New Catholic Encyclopedia*, ed. Berard L. Marthaler, 2nd ed. (Detroit: Thomson/Gale in association with The Catholic University of America, 2003), vol. 5, 636.
11 Tom Junod, "The Falling Man: An Unforgettable Story," *Esquire*, 9 September 2021, https://www.esquire.com/news-politics/a48031/the-falling-man-tom-junod/. Thanks to Bryan McLennan for sharing this article with me.
12 Gaius Suetonius Tranquillus, *The Twelve Caesars* (121 CE), trans. Robert Graves (1957); rev. trans. James Rives (London: Penguin Classics, 2007). See also Francesca Leaf, "The Emperor, the Usurper, and the Stuck Eagle," *Classical Wisdom Weekly*, 25 February 2015, https://classicalwisdom.com/emperor-usurper-stuck-eagle.

13 Albert Camus, *The Myth of Sisyphus and Other Essays* (1955), trans. Justin O'Brien, 2nd ed. (New York: Vintage International, 2018), 121, 123.

14 Ibid., 123.

15 See Anil Ananthaswamy, "Cosmic Countdown," *New Scientist* 3239 (20 July 2019): 34–7.

16 Daniel McCoy, "Ragnarok," https://norse-mythology.org/tales/ragnarok. See also further discussion of the Norse view of fate in Neil Price, *The Children of Ash and Elm: A History of the Vikings* (London: Allen Lane, 2020), 50–1. Thanks to Rob Banks for suggesting this second reference.

17 Bolle, "Fate," 3004.

18 *Bhagavad Gita*, chap. 11, verse 32, Bhagavad Gita Online; https://srimad bhagavadgita.net. According to many sources, J. Robert Oppenheimer (1904– 1967), the American physicist who led the original atomic bomb research, recalled and/or recited this verse when witnessing the first successful test explosion in the New Mexican desert in July 1945, rendering it as: "Now I am become Death, the destroyer of worlds."

19 While many philosophers have agonized over death and dying, E.M. Cioran is one who's obsessed with the problem of birth; see *The Trouble with Being Born*, trans. Richard Howard (New York: Arcade, 2012).

20 Gelven, *Why Me?*, 28 (emphasis in original).

21 Martin Heidegger, *Being and Time* (first pub. 1927), trans. John Macquarrie and Edward Robinson (New York: Harper Perennial, 2008).

22 Plato, *Phaedo* (c. 380–360 BCE), trans. David Gallop (Oxford: Oxford University Press, 2009). This dialogue recounts Socrates' doctrine of the soul and immortality and allegedly takes place on the day he was put to death for his beliefs (in 399 BCE).

23 *The Tibetan Book of the Dead*, trans. Gyurme Dorje, Graham Coleman, and Thupten Jinpa; intro. commentary His Holiness the Dalai Lama (New York: Viking Penguin, 2006). Original title: *Bardo Thodol*, composed by Buddhist master Padmasambhava and written down by one of his students. The edition referenced here is said to be "the first complete translation."

24 Gerald Murnane, *Inland* (first pub. 1988) (Artarmon, NSW, Ausralia: Giramondo, 2013), 241.

25 Molière, *The Physician in Spite of Himself* (1666), trans. Brett B. Bodemer, 2011, https://digitalcommons.calpoly.edu/cgi/viewcontent.cgi?referer =https://www.google.com/&httpsredir=1&article=1077&context=lib_fac.

26 Søren Kierkegaard, *Concluding Unscientific Postscript to the Philosophical Crumbs* (1846), ed. and trans. Alastair Hannay (Cambridge: Cambridge University Press, 2009), 171.

27 The term figures most prominently in phenomenology and existentialism, for example as used by Edmund Husserl (1859–1938), Martin Heidegger, Jean-Paul Sartre, and Simone de Beauvoir (1908–1986).
28 Rachel Cusk, *Outline* (London: Faber & Faber, 2014), 161.
29 Ibid., 162.
30 Dominic Smith, *The Electric Hotel* (Sydney: Allen & Unwin, 2019), 288, 329.
31 Stan Grant, *Talking to My Country* (Sydney: HarperCollins, 2017), 73.
32 Eilstein, *Life Contemplative, Life Practical*, 152–3.
33 Michael J. Fox, as quoted in Allen Klein, *You Can't Ruin My Day: 52 Wake-Up Calls to Turn Any Situation Around* (New York: Viva Editions, 2015), 29.
34 Lao Tzu, *The Tao Te Ching*, trans. Brian Browne Walker (New York: St Martin's Griffin, 1995), verses 1, 4.
35 Stephen R. Bokenkamp, "Daoism: An Overview," in *New Catholic Encyclopedia*, ed. Berard L. Marthaler, second edition (Detroit: Thomson/Gale in association with the Catholic University of America, 2003), vol. 4, 2177.
36 Friedrich Nietzsche, *The Gay Science* (1882), trans. Walter Kaufmann (New York: Vintage Books, 1974), sec. 276, 223.
37 See Nietzsche, *The Gay Science*; and Friedrich Nietzsche, *Thus Spoke Zarathustra: A Book for Everyone and Nobody* (written 1883–85), trans. Graham Parkes (Oxford: Oxford University Press, 2005).
38 Friedrich Nietzsche, *The Will to Power* (pub. posthumously in 1901 and 1906), trans. Walter Kaufmann and R.J. Hollingdale (New York: Vintage Books, 1968), sec. 1041 (written 1888), 536–7.
39 See subtitle of *Ecce Homo*, note 37 below.
40 See, for example, Jared Keller, "The Psychology (and Philosophy) of 'No Regrets,'" *Pacific Standard*, 14 June 2017, https://psmag.com/social-justice/its-our-party-we-can-do-what-we-want-until-we-die-so-lead-a-meaningful-life-okay. For an example of a distinguished contemporary thinker who was deeply influenced by Nietzsche's amor fati ideal, see Joseph Campbell, *Reflections on the Art of Living: A Joseph Campbell Companion*, ed. Diane K. Osbon (New York: HarperCollins, 1991).
41 Friedrich Nietzsche, *Ecce Homo: How One Becomes What One Is* (written 1888, first published 1908), "Why I Am So Clever," sec. 10, trans. R.J. Hollingdale (London: Penguin Books, 1992), 37–8 (emphasis in original).
42 Cahn, *Fate, Logic, and Time*, 9 (emphases in original).

AFTERWORD

1 With a grateful nod to Gabriel García Márquez (1927–2014), *Love in the Time of Cholera*, trans. Edith Grossman (New York: Alfred A. Knopf, 1985).

2 Hannah Devlin, "Road to a Cure: A Vaccine Is Our Only Hope. What Are the Chances for Its Success?" *Guardian Weekly*, 1 May 2020, 18.

3 Sumit Paul-Choudhury, "Tomorrow's Gods: What Is the Future of Religion?," BBC Future, 2 August 2019, http://www.bbc.com/future/story/20190801-tomorrows-gods-what-is-the-future-of-religion.

4 Intisār-al-Haq, "Fatalism," *Islamic Studies* 8 (1969): 245.

RECOMMENDED READING

Ackerman, Jennifer G. *Chance in the House of Fate: A Natural History of Heredity*. London: Bloomsbury, 2001.

Alexander of Aphrodisias. *Alexander of Aphrodisias on Fate* (*To the Emperors on Fate and Responsibility* [c. 200 CE]), edited and translated by R.W. Sharples. London: Duckworth, 1983.

Bargdill, Richard W. "Fate and Destiny: Some Historical Distinctions between the Concepts." *Journal of Theoretical and Philosophical Psychology* 26 (2006): 205–20, https://www.researchgate.net/publication/232606852_Fate_and_destiny_Some_historical_distinctions_between_the_concepts.

Bernstein, Mark. *Fatalism*. Lincoln: University of Nebraska Press, 1992.

Bolle, Kees W. "Fate." In *Encyclopedia of Religion*, 2nd ed., edited by Lindsay Jones, volume 5, 2998–3006. Detroit: Macmillan Reference USA/Thomson Gale, 2005.

Borland, Tully. "Omniscience and Divine Foreknowledge." In *Internet Encyclopedia of Philosophy*, 2022, edited by James Fieser and Bradley Dowden, https://www.iep.utm.edu/omnisci.

Bourne, C. "Fatalism and the Future." In *The Oxford Handbook of Philosophy of Time*, edited by C. Callender, 41–67. Oxford: Oxford University Press, 2011.

Brennan, Tad. *The Stoic Life: Emotions, Duties, and Fate*. Oxford: Clarendon Press, 2007.

Brouwer, René, and Emmanuele Vimercati, eds. *Fate, Providence and Free Will: Philosophy and Religion in Dialogue in the Early Imperial Age*. Leiden: Brill, 2020.

Cahn, Steven M. *Fate, Logic, and Time*. New Haven: Yale University Press, 1967. (Republished Eugene, OR: Resource Publications, 2004.)

Carroll, Sean B. *A Series of Fortunate Events: Chance and the Making of the Planet, Life, and You*. Princeton: Princeton University Press, 2020.

Cicero. *On Fate* (44 BCE) and Boethius, *The Consolation of Philosophy IV.5–7 and V*, edited and translated by R.W. Sharples. Liverpool: Liverpool University Press, 1991. Also available, translated by H. Rackham, at http://www.informationphilosopher.com.

Cohen-Mor, Dalya. *A Matter of Fate: The Concept of Fate in the Arab World as Reflected in Modern Arabic Literature*. Oxford: Oxford University Press, 2001.

Critchlow, Hannah. *The Science of Fate: Why Your Future Is More Predictable Than You Think*. London: Hodder & Stoughton, 2019.

Dorner, A. et al. "Fate." In *Encyclopaedia of Religion and Ethics*, edited by James Hastings, volume 5, 771–96. Edinburgh: T&T Clark, 1912.

Eidinow, Esther. *Luck, Fate and Fortune: Antiquity and Its Legacy*. Oxford: Oxford University Press, 2011.

Eilstein, Helena. *Life Contemplative, Life Practical: An Essay on Fatalism*. Amsterdam: Rodopi, 1997.

Evans, Gavin. *Skin Deep: Journeys in the Divisive Science of Race*. London: Oneworld Publications, 2019.

Fischer, John Martin, and Patrick Todd, eds. *Freedom, Fatalism, and Foreknowledge*. New York: Oxford University Press, 2015.

Garrett, Brian. "Fatalism: A Dialogue." *Think: Philosophy for Everyone* 17 (2018): 73–9.

Gelven, Michael. *Why Me?: A Philosophical Inquiry into Fate*. DeKalb, IL: Northern Illinois University Press, 1991.

Gray, Louis Herbert, and George Foot Moore, eds. *The Mythology of All Races*, 13 volumes. New York: Cooper Square Publishers, 1964.

Hales, Steven D. *The Myth of Luck: Philosophy, Fate, and Fortune*. London: Bloomsbury Academic, 2020.

Hawking, Stephen. *The Theory of Everything: The Origin and Fate of the Universe*, special edition. Beverly Hills: Phoenix Books, 2006.

Kingwell, Mark. *On Risk*. Windsor: Biblioasis, 2020.

Linden, David. *Unique: The New Science of Human Individuality*. New York: Basic Books, 2020.

Lucas, John Randolph. *The Future: An Essay on God, Temporality, and Truth*. Oxford: Blackwell, 1989.

Mack, Katie. *The End of Everything (Astrophysically Speaking)*. New York: Scribner, 2020.

Onians, R.B. *The Origins of European Thought: About the Body, the Mind, the Soul, the World, Time and Fate*. Cambridge: Cambridge University Press, 1951.

Pike, Nelson. "Divine Omniscience and Voluntary Action." *Philosophical Review* 74 (1965): 27–46.

Rice, Hugh. "Fatalism." In *Stanford Encyclopedia of Philosophy*, 23 February 2023 revision, edited by Edward N. Zalta, https://plato.stanford.edu/entries/fatalism.

Sanford, John A. *Fate, Love, and Ecstasy: Wisdom from the Lesser-Known Goddesses of the Greeks.* Asheville, NC: Chiron, 1995.

Sider, Ted, and Earl Conee. *Riddles of Existence: A Guided Tour of Metaphysics*, new edition. Oxford: Oxford University Press, 2014.

Small, Robin. "Fatalism and Deliberation." *Canadian Journal of Philosophy* 18 (1988): 13–30.

Solomon, Robert C. "Nietzsche as Existentialist and as Fatalist: The Practical Paradoxes of Self-Making." *International Studies in Philosophy* 34 (2002): 41–54.

Swartz, Norman. "Foreknowledge and Free Will." In *Internet Encyclopedia of Philosophy*, 2022, edited by James Fieser and Bradley Dowden, https://www.iep.utm.edu/foreknow/#H8.

Taylor, Richard. *Metaphysics*, 4th ed. Englewood Cliffs, NJ: Prentice-Hall, 1992.

Uslander, Arlene, and Brenda Warneka, eds. *The Simple Touch of Fate: How the Hand of Fate Touched Our Lives Forever – Real People, Real Stories.* New York: iUniverse, 2003.

Thalberg, Irving. "Fatalism toward Past and Future." In *Time and Cause: Essays Presented to Richard Taylor*, edited by Peter van Inwagen, 27–47. Dordrecht: Dordrecht Reidel, 1980.

Visser, Margaret. *Beyond Fate.* CBC Massey Lectures. Toronto: House of Anansi Press, 2002.

Wallace, David Foster. *Fate, Time, and Language: An Essay on Free Will*, reprint edition. New York: Columbia University Press, 2010.

Wei, Yixia. *The Chinese Philosophy of Fate.* Translated by Weidong Wang. Singapore: Springer Nature, 2017.

White, Heath. *Fate and Free Will: A Defense of Theological Determinism.* Notre Dame, IN: University of Notre Dame Press, 2019.

Wilkerson, Isabel. *Caste: The Origins of Our Discontents.* New York: Penguin Random House, 2020.

INDEX